Discover ...

Topics for Advanced Learners
Series Editor: Klaus Hinz

The Australian Aboriginals

Teachers' Book

By Elsa Zettelmann-Kunde

Schöningh Verlag

Sprachliche Betreuung: James Martin

www.schoeningh-schulbuch.de
Schöningh Verlag, Jühenplatz 1–3, 33098 Paderborn

Druck A [7 6 5] / Jahr 2008 07 06
Alle Drucke der Serie A sind im Unterricht parallel verwendbar.
Die letzte Zahl bezeichnet das Jahr dieses Druckes.

Umschlaggestaltung: Veronika Wypior
Druck und Bindung: AZ Druck und Datentechnik GmbH/Kempten (Allgäu)

ISBN 13: 978-3-14-040062-6
ISBN 10: 3-14-040062-4

Inhaltsverzeichnis

Discover ... : Zielsetzung und methodischer Ansatz

Die Themenheftreihe Discover... richtet sich an Schülerinnen und Schüler der Sekundarstufe II und bereitet in Anlehnung an den Themenkatalog der Richtlinien Englisch landeskundliche oder allgemeine, Jugendliche interessierende Themen methodisch-didaktisch auf. Die Verfahrensweise lehnt sich an neuere lernpsychologische Erkenntnisse an. Das besondere Merkmal liegt in der Bearbeitung der Texte anhand von *pre-reading-, while-reading-* und *post-reading*-Aufgaben.

Pre-reading-Aufgaben führen zum Text, Thema oder Problem hin. Forschungsergebnisse belegen, dass eine interessante Texteröffnung einen positiven Einfluss auf die Textbegegnung hat. Die *pre-reading*-Aufgaben konkretisieren zudem besonders das Vorwissen und bauen Erwartungshaltungen auf. Spezifische *pre-reading*-Aufgaben finden sich in Form von Bild/Text-Collagen auf der in ein Kapitel einführenden „Start here"-Seite.

Beim ersten fortlaufenden Lesen kommen unterschiedliche textverarbeitende Operationen ins Spiel. Da hierzu in der Regel nur begrenzte Zeit zur Verfügung steht, ist eine Hilfstätigkeit darin zu sehen, beim Lesen von Zeit zu Zeit innezuhalten um auf das bereits Gelesene zurückzublicken. Durch das verlangsamte Lesetempo können intensivere Interaktionen zwischen Leser und Text stattfinden. Reflexions- und Verstehenshilfen finden sich in *Discover...* in den *while-reading*-Aufgaben und Beobachtungsanleitungen in der Randspalte. Sie begleiten den Lesevorgang und dienen gleichsam als *navigational aid*. Mit ihrer Hilfe wird das Verständnis der Oberflächenstruktur des Textes sichergestellt. Diese methodische Neuheit wird durch ein besonderes Layout, durch die Unterteilung der Seite in eine Textspalte und eine die *white-reading*-Aufgaben enthaltene Randspalte ermöglicht. Die mit Pfeilen versehenen Aufgaben begleiten den Lesevorgang. Sie haben vorwärtsweisenden, rückverweisenden oder statarischen Charakter. Ein nach unten weisender Pfeil (⮟) verknüpft die Aufgabe mit dem nachfolgenden Text als so genannte Beobachtungsanleitung. Eine mit einem nach innen gerichteten Pfeil (⮜) versehene Aufgabe bezieht sich auf die betreffende Textstelle und ein nach oben weisender Pfeil (⮝) zeigt an, dass sich die Aufgabe auf den gerade gelesenen Textteil bezieht und man sich rückblickend Klarheit über das Textverständnis verschaffen soll.

Alternativ zum *guided reading* können die Aufgaben der Randspalte auch erst nach dem Lesen mündlich oder schriftlich beantwortet werden; ihnen kommt dann die Funktion der üblichen *comprehension questions* zur Überprüfung des Textverständnisses zu. In diesem Fall überlesen die Schüler während des ersten Durchgangs die Fragen und Aufgaben zunächst.

Die sich an den Text anschließenden *Activities* sind vertiefender Natur. Sie beziehen sich auf die kreative Textproduktion sowie auf die Interpretation im weitesten Sinn. Damit wird auch der textanalytische Zugriff geschult.

Die Kombination von *pre-reading-, while-reading-* und *after-reding-assignments (activities)* ermöglicht eine an neuesten lernpsychologischen und methodischen Erkenntnissen orientierte Textbearbeitung im Sinne einer vermittelnden Methode, bei der Leser und Text gleichermaßen den ihnen zukommenden Stellenwert erhalten.

Klaus Hinz

Teil I

Discover ... The Australian Aboriginals:
Die didaktische Konzeption

Die didaktische Konzeption

Das Thema "The Australian Aboriginals" im Englischunterricht

Der vorliegende Reader richtet sich an Schülerinnen und Schüler der Oberstufe und kann innerhalb der Obligatorik von Lerninhalten zum Thema *Minoritäten* eingesetzt werden. Er mag als Alternative zu den üblichen Themenfeldern (z.B. Black Americans, North American Indians etc.), die auch von Lehrerinnen und Lehrern anderer Fächer „abgeerntet“ werden, willkommen sein. Einzelne Teile können auch im Zusammenhang mit der Lehrbucheinheit über Australien, die in den gängigen Lehrwerken für die Jahrgangstufe 9 vorgesehen ist, eingesetzt werden.
Die sechs chronologisch aufeinander aufbauenden Kapitel vermitteln einen Einblick in das Leben der indigenen Australier, beginnend mit der Zeit vor der Ankunft der Weißen. Es folgt die Darstellung der weiteren Phasen im konfliktreichen Zusammenleben mit den europäischen Australiern bis hin zum Versuch der Versöhnung und dem Streben nach einem friedlichen Bikulturalismus. Obwohl die Urbevölkerung das Zentrum des Interesses bildet, werden gesamtaustralische Zusammenhänge berücksichtigt und Hintergrundereignisse beleuchtet, wo dies zum Verständnis der Entwicklung notwendig ist.
Die Textsammlung spiegelt vorrangig die Sicht der indigenen Australier wider. Dabei greifen in den einzelnen Kapiteln Texte unterschiedlicher Herkunft und Art themenbezogen ineinander. In den späteren Kapiteln kommt zunehmend auch die Perspektive der Weißen zum Tragen, sodass ein breites Meinungsspektrum entsteht.
Die den Texten folgenden *Activities* enthalten u.a. Aufgaben, die die Schülerinnen und Schüler zur kritischen Meinungsbildung und -äußerung auffordern und sie ermuntern sich themenübergreifend zu informieren und größere Gesamtzusammenhänge herzustellen.
Nach unserem Verständnis fallen die australischen Ureinwohner unter den Begriff „minorities“ und können in der Oberstufe in Zusammenhang mit der Minoritätenproblematik behandelt werden. Fragte man die Betroffenen selber, so würden sie sich weder als „minority“ noch als „problem“ sehen. Sie würden vielmehr auf das „Majoritätenproblem“ verweisen, das sie mit der in ihr Land gekommenen weißen Mehrheit haben.
Minoritäten entstehen durch Anderssein. Das Collins English Dictionary definiert „minority“ als „a group that is different racially, politically, etc. from a larger group of which it is a part“. Die Definition macht das Trennende aber auch das Gemeinsame deutlich. Warum aber wird dem Anderssein so große Bedeutung zugemessen, dass es zur Schaffung ausgrenzender Begriffe führt? Die Auseinandersetzung mit dieser Frage bildet einen thematischen Schwerpunkt des Readers.
Es mag für die Schülerinnen und Schüler interessant sein zu erfahren, wie es den indigenen Australiern seit Ankunft der ersten britischen Flotte ergangen ist. Einige werden beim Lesen der Texte mit ungläubigem Staunen oder mit Betroffenheit reagieren. Dies allein wäre nicht Rechtfertigung genug für den Einsatz eines ganzen Themenheftes.

Am Beispiel des Konfliktes zwischen indigenen und nicht-indigenen Australiern können die Schülerinnen und Schüler grundlegende Erkenntnisse über ihr eigenes Verhalten im Umgang mit anderen Menschen gewinnen, indem sie dieses reflektieren, einordnen, bewerten und bestenfalls verändern. Sie sind aufgefordert, ihr Wertesystem und ihre Toleranzfähigkeit zu überprüfen und sich immer wieder erneut die Frage zu stellen, welche Meinung sie in einer gegebenen Situation vertreten und welche Handlungsstrategien sie daraus entwickeln würden.
In unserer zunehmend multikulturellen Gesellschaft sind wir ständig mit dem Anderssein unserer Mitmenschen konfrontiert. Wie reagieren wir darauf? Irritiert uns der Umgang mit Menschen aus anderen Kulturkreisen, die ihr Anderssein nicht verhehlen, oder nehmen wir ihr Aussehen und Verhalten ohne Bewertung zur Kenntnis? Denken wir automatisch, dass es doch eigentlich besser für sie wäre, wenn sie unsere Vorstellungen teilten? Die Wahrscheinlichkeit, dass wir uns irren, wenn wir unser Wertesystem auf andere Kulturen übertragen, ist eher groß. Dies gilt auch für die Übertragung eigener Wertvorstellungen auf unsere Mitmenschen, die zu Enttäuschung und Frustration auf beiden Seiten führen kann.
Ein Teil des Readers setzt sich schwerpunktmäßig mit diesem Aspekt auseinander. Auch hier sollen die Schülerinnen und Schüler, ausgehend von der Situation der indigenen Australier, den Bezug zu ihrem Erfahrungshorizont herstellen. Dabei kann es hilfreich sein, dass der Gegenstand der Betrachtung ein sehr weit entfernt liegender ist und dass die ersten weißen Australier nicht Deutsche waren, denn es scheint leichter zu sein, das Fehlverhalten anderer kritisch zu betrachten als das eigene.
Schließlich dürfte sich die Tatsache, dass die Schülerinnen und Schüler Einblick in eine Kultur gewinnen, deren bloße Existenz bei uns bisher wenig bekannt ist, motivierend auswirken. Vielleicht darf in Abwandlung des Textes „Two-Ways Strong“ gesagt werden: Learning about different cultures makes you become „more-ways strong“.

Textauswahl

Die ersten Kapitel dieses Themenheftes sollen eine Vorstellung davon vermitteln, wer die Menschen waren, die so lange vor Ankunft der Europäer auf dem australischen Kontinent gelebt hatten, welches Selbstverständnis sie hatten und welchen Platz sie innerhalb der Welt einnahmen, in die plötzlich unbekannte Wesen eindrangen, um ihnen die Souveränität über ihr Land zu nehmen.
Der Zugang zu dem indigenen Kulturgut wird dadurch erschwert, dass die Aborigines nicht über das geschriebene Wort verfügten, sondern ihre Geschichte(n) mündlich tradierten und zwar in vielen verschiedenen Stammessprachen. Mit dem Streben nach Unabhängigkeit und Selbstverwaltung wuchs auch der Wunsch, die eigene Geschichte zu erhalten und schriftlich zu fixieren, solange es noch „elders“ gab, die die „legends“ kannten. „Aboriginal history is Australian history“ hieß es nun. Der 1980 erschienene Sammelband *Australian Dreaming* setzte den Trend als „the first Aboriginal history of the Australian continent and its people, as told by the Aboriginal story-tellers.“

Es widerstrebt europäischem Forschergeist gründlich, dass das „Aboriginal secret business“ an Nichtinitiierte nicht weitergegeben wird. Wandjuk Marika, Gründungsmitglied und zeitweiliger Vorsitzender des *Aboriginal Arts Board of the Australia Council* sagt im Vorwort zu *Australian Dreaming*: "In the areas where my people are still leading their traditional life our legends are strong and our history can be told today, just as my father taught me and his father and grandfather the same before that. We want to tell you our story, not the inner secrets of our deepest beliefs – these we keep sacred for our generations to come so that our culture can remain whole – but the story as we tell it to our young people before they become initiated into the sacred Law."

(*Australian Dreaming. 40,000 Years of Aboriginal History,* compiled and edited by Jennifer Isaacs, Willoughby, Ure Smith Press, 1991, p. 5)

Die Texte sind thematisch so aufeinander aufgebaut, dass sie den Schülerinnen und Schülern Wissen und Einsichten vermitteln, die sie zu einer eigenen Meinungsbildung befähigen sollten. Dabei kommt es weniger darauf an, dass sie eindeutige Lösungsvorschläge machen, als dass sie eine differenzierte Sicht erlangen.

In formaler Hinsicht folgt die Textauswahl dem Prinzip der Darstellung eines Sachverhaltes in einem expositorischen Text und seiner folgenden literarischen Verarbeitung, wo dies angebracht scheint und möglich ist. Die fiktionalen Texte greifen die vorher gegebenen Sachinformationen in individualisierter Form auf und ermöglichen den Lernenden den affektiven Zugang zur Textproblematik.

Tabellarische Textübersicht

Autor, Text	Inhaltliche Schwerpunkte	Textsorte	Wortzahl
	Chapter 1: Life in Perfect Isolation – The Beginning		
Jennifer Isaacs, *The Arrival of the First Australians*	• Der australische Kontinent vor 40.000 Jahren • Vermutungen über die Herkunft der ersten Australier	nichtfiktional (Auszug aus einer Geschichtsdarstellung aus Sicht der indigenen Australier)	328
Jennifer Isaacs, *The Creation Era*	• Die Schöpfungsgeschichte und ihre Auswirkungen auf das Leben der Aborigines • „Dreamtime“ und „Dreaming“	nichtfiktional (Auszug aus einer Geschichtsdarstellung aus Sicht der indigenen Australier)	297
Jennifer Isaacs, *The Desert Ancestors*	• Das Vermächtnis der „Great Ancestors“	nichtfiktional (Auszug aus einer Geschichtsdarstellung aus Sicht der indigenen Australier)	133
Bill Neidjie, *Law*	• Die Bedeutung des „Aboriginal Law“	Aufzeichnung der gesprochenen Worte von Bill Neidjie	47

Autor, Text	Inhaltliche Schwerpunkte	Textsorte	Wortzahl
Chapter 2: The Arrival of the Pale-Skinned Strangers – The Invasion			
Jennifer Isaacs, *The Invaders*	• Die Ankunft der ersten englischen Flotte in Botany Bay im Jahre 1788 • Die Auswirkungen dieses Ereignisses auf die Urbevölkerung	nichtfiktional (Auszug aus einer Geschichtsdarstellung aus Sicht der indigenen Australier)	443
Terra Nullius	• Die *Terra Nullius*-Doktrin als Rechtfertigung für die Landnahme im Namen der Krone	nichtfiktional (Auszug aus *The Encyclopaedia of Aboriginal Australia*)	198
Robert Hughes, *First Encounters – Value Clashes*	• Die indigenen Australier aus der Sicht der ersten Weißen	nichtfiktional (Auszug aus einer Geschichtsdarstellung)	430
Hyllus Maris, *Spiritual Song of the Aborigine*	• Das spirituelle Selbstverständnis der Aborigines	fiktional (Gedicht)	122
Jennifer Isaacs, *The Vengeance of the Spirit Ancestors*	• Der Zorn der „Great Ancestors" über die Entweihung sakraler Stätten äußert sich in Naturkatastrophen • Beispiel einer Konfliktsituation	nichtfiktional (Auszug aus einer Geschichtsdarstellung aus Sicht der indigenen Australier)	459
Bill Neidjie, *Land*	• Der Tabu-Charakter der „sacred sites" • Folgen bei Missachtung	Aufzeichnung der gesprochenen Worte von Bill Neidjie	106
Bill Neidjie / Stephen Davis / Allan Fox, *Big Bill Neidjie*	• Vergleich der Worte von Chief Seattle über die Bedeutung des Landes mit Bill Neidjies „story"	nichtfiktional (Klappentext)	203
Chapter 3: "They Were Not Fit to Live within the General Community" – From Protection to Assimilation			
Protectors of Aborigines	• Die „Protection"-Phase: Ziele, praktische Umsetzung und Folgen für die indigenen Australier	nichtfiktional (Auszug aus *The Encyclopaedia of Aboriginal Australia)*	232
Selma Sampson Nampijinpa, *The Girl Who Was Taken Away from Her Family*	• Die Auswirkungen der „Protection Laws" auf das Leben der „part-Aboriginals" • Ihre Schutzlosigkeit gegenüber den Weißen	fiktional (Kurzdrama)	657
Oh Don't You Wish that You Were Me	• Ethnozentrismus	fiktional (Kindergedicht)	116

Autor, Text	Inhaltliche Schwerpunkte	Textsorte	Wortzahl
"Love White Men and Learn to Speak English"	• Assimilation • Ethnozentrismus • *stolen generation*	nichtfiktional (Auszug aus *The Encyclopaedia of Aboriginal Australia)*	251
Bob Randall, *Brown Skin Baby*	• Das Wehklagen einer schwarzen Mutter, deren Kind zwangsweise ins Heim gebracht wurde	fiktional (Gedicht)	172
Glenyse Ward, *Wandering Girl – Unna You Fullas*	• Das Leben in einem von deutschen Missionaren geführten Waisenhaus • Die Einstellung der Missionare zu den „Waisenkindern" • Die von den Missionaren verfolgten Ziele	fiktional (Romanauszug)	714
"Link-Up" Wants to Help"	• *Link-Up* hilft Betroffenen der *stolen generation* und ihren Familien bei der Zusammenführung	Broschüre	126
Oodgeroo Noonuccal, *Assimilation – No! Integration – Yes!*	• Ablehnung von Assimilation • Befürwortung von Integration und Bikulturalismus	fiktional (Gedicht)	155

Chapter 4: "Aboriginals Are a People, Not a Minority" – On the Way to Self-Management

Autor, Text	Inhaltliche Schwerpunkte	Textsorte	Wortzahl
From Protection to Self-Management	• Die Politik, die die australische Bundesregierung und die einzelnen Staaten bezüglich der Aborigines verfolgten, gliedert sich in 4 Phasen: *protection, assimilation, integration, self-management*	nichtfiktional (Auszug aus *The Encyclopaedia of Aboriginal Australia)*	256
The Torres Strait Islanders and Their New Flag	• Die Torres Strait Islanders als Teil der „Australian Indigenous Peoples" • Die neue Flagge der Torres Strait Islanders als Symbol ihrer inneren Einheit	nichtfiktional (Artikel aus *ATSIC-News)*	108
Monica Foxwell, *Love and Marriage*	• Die Leserbriefschreiberin vergleicht die Einbürgerung mit einer Eheschließung • Sie schlägt vor den Union Jack auf der australischen Flagge durch die *Aboriginal Flag* zu ersetzen	nichtfiktional (Leserbrief aus *The Bulletin with Newsweek)*	114
Traumatic Experience versus Opportunity to Develop	• Die Trennung von den Eltern und die Erziehung im Heim als Basis für eine Künstlerkarriere	nichtfiktional (Artikel aus *ATSIC-News)*	99
David McNicoll, *Gratitude Wanted*	• Der Kolumnist beklagt die Undankbarkeit einiger Aborigines, die die gut gemeinten Angebote der weißen Australier verschmähen	nichtfiktional (Kolumne aus *The Bulletin with Newsweek)*	142
Michael Polya, *"They Have Every Reason to Be Grateful"*	• Die Erziehung in Heimen hat den Angehörigen der *stolen generation* Karrieren eröffnet, die ihnen sonst verschlossen geblieben wären • Die Aborigines sind den weißen Australiern zu Dank verpflichtet für die Verbesserung ihrer Lebensbedingungen seit Ankunft der 1. Flotte	nichtfiktional (Leserbrief aus *The Bulletin with Newsweek)*	157

Autor, Text	Inhaltliche Schwerpunkte	Textsorte	Wort-zahl
Nene Gare, *The Fringe Dwellers*	• Literarische Verarbeitung des Dankbarkeitsmotivs • Das Zusammenleben schwarzer und weißer Australier in so genannten „mixed areas“	fiktional (Romanauszug)	1113
Chapter 5: Walking Together – The Reconciliation Process			
Diana Bagnall, *Pat Dodson – A Creative Mind*	• Kurzbiografie von Pat Dodson • Dodsons Vorstellungen von „reconciliation“	nichtfiktional (Artikel aus *The Bulletin with Newsweek)*	267
Mabo and the Fight for Native Title	• Die Bedeutung des *Mabo Case* für die Landrechts-Bewegung • Das Urteil des Obersten Gerichtshofes vom 3.6.1992	nichtfiktional (Zeitungsartikel)	235
The “Wik Case”	• Verpachtetes Land ist von Native Title-Forderungen nicht ausgeschlossen • Die Auswirkungen des *Wik*-Urteils	nichtfiktional (Autorentext)	318
Brendon Bowes, *Grave-Robbing in Tasmania*	• Grabschändungen mit Zustimmung der tasmanischen Regierung • Das Interesse der Museen an den sterblichen Überresten der letzten indigenen Tasmanier • Der Einfluss des Darwinismus auf das Verhalten der Wissenschaftler	nichtfiktional (Artikel aus *The Bulletin with Newsweek)*	887
Bill Neidjie, *Death*	• Bill Neidjie sagt mit seinen Worten, wie wichtig es ist, dass die Toten am richtigen Ort begraben werden	Aufzeichnung der gesprochenen Worte von Bill Neidjie	49
Aboriginal Remains Back Where They Belong	• Die Rückführung der sterblichen Überreste indigener Australier aus der Universität Edinburgh • Die Bedeutung dieses Ereignisses für die heute lebenden Aborigines • Die Bestattung der sterblichen Überreste am richtigen Ort	nichtfiktional (Artikel aus *ATSIC-News)*	318
Living Black in a White Society	• Während die weißen Australier am 26. Januar ihren „Australia Day“ begehen, feiern die Aborigines an diesem Tag in Gegenveranstaltungen das Überleben ihrer Kultur	nichtfiktional (Zeitungsartikel)	61
Chapter 6: “Put Two and Two Together” – Becoming “Two-Ways Strong”			
Kerry-Anne Walsh, *The Double Life of Bruce Martin – Thorough Biculturalism*	• Gelebter Bikulturalismus: ein Public-School-Schüler aus Canberra nimmt in den Ferien am Stammesleben der Familie seiner Mutter in Nordqueensland teil • Der Schüler sieht einen Gewinn darin, in zwei verschiedenen Welten leben zu können	nichtfiktional (Artikel aus *The Bulletin with Newsweek)*	609
“Two-Ways Strong”	• Bikulturalismus als Chance für eine bessere Bildung • Bildung als Mittel um den Teufelskreis der Armut zu durchbrechen	nichtfiktional (Auszug aus *The Encyclopaedia of Aboriginal Australia)*	235

Autor, Text	Inhaltliche Schwerpunkte	Textsorte	Wort-zahl
Peter Wear, *The Exhausted Optimist*	• Der Gegensatz Nord-Süd • Ein „erschöpfter“ Aktivist aus der Landrechts-Bewegung wendet sich seiner persönlichen Karriere zu • Seine Kindheit in einer protestantischen Mission • Noel Pearson, ein Beispiel für „becoming two-ways strong“	nichtfiktional (Artikel aus *The Bulletin with Newsweek)*	443
Adam Stout, *A Letter from England*	• Der „englische Briefschreiber“ wartet seit 7 Jahren vergeblich auf die von Burnum Burnum angekündigte Besetzung seines Landes • „Two-Ways Strong“ mit umgekehrtem Vorzeichen: der Briefschreiber ist der Meinung, dass die Europäer von den indigenen Australiern lernen können ihre Umwelt zu erhalten	„Leserbrief“ (aus *The Koori Mail)*	499
Bill Neidjie, *Conclusion*	• Bill Neidjie kommt zu dem Schluss, dass alle Menschen, ungeachtet ihrer Hautfarbe und Sprache, die gleichen Gefühle haben und dass sie ihr Menschsein miteinander verbindet	Aufzeichnung der gesprochenen Worte von Bill Neidjie	41

Integration des Heftes in größere thematische Zusammenhänge

Ein nicht zu übersehendes Problem bei der Erstellung eines solchen Themenheftes liegt in der notwendigen Eingrenzung des Gegenstandes. So werden die Schülerinnen und Schüler am Ende des Kurses möglicherweise sagen, dass sie jetzt einiges über die Aborigines wissen, kaum aber etwas über Australien. Aus diesem Grund eignet sich das Thema ganz besonders zum *Team Teaching*. Dies wiederum ist in der Oberstufe nicht leicht zu organisieren. Dennoch sollten Englischlehrerinnen und -lehrer, die beabsichtigen mit ihrem Kurs die indigenen Australier zu „entdecken“, versuchen Religions-, Biologie-, Erdkunde-, Geschichtslehrer etc. für ihr Anliegen zu gewinnen, damit sie mit auf Entdeckungsreise gehen.

Weiterführende Literatur

Allgemeine Informationen über Australien:

- Margaret Nicholson: *The Little Aussie Fact Book*, Ringwood, Penguin Books Australia Ltd, 5th ed. 1993

Die Geschichte der „convicts“ und die Anfänge der Strafkolonie Australien:

- Robert Hughes: *The Fatal Shore*, London, Pan Books Ltd, 1988

Einführung in die Kultur der Aborigines:

- Cyril Havecker: *Understanding Aboriginal Culture*, ed. by Yvonne Malykke, Sydney, Cosmos Periodicals, 1987
- *Aboriginal Australia. An Introductory Reader in Aboriginal Studies*, ed. by Colin Bourke, Eleanor Bourke and Bill Edwards, St Lucia, University of Queensland Press, 1994

Dokumentation über die „stolen generation“:

- Barbara Cummings: *Take This Child ...*, Canberra, Aboriginal Studies Press, 1990

Romane/autobiografische Romane:

- Sally Morgan: *My Place*, South Fremantle, Fremantle Arts Centre Press, 1987
- Sally Morgan: *Wanamurraganya*, South Fremantle, Fremantle Arts Centre Press, 1989
- Glenyse Ward: *Wandering Girl*, Broome, Magabala Books, 1987
- Glenyse Ward: *Unna You Fullas*, Broome, Magabala Books, 1991
- Nene Gare: *The Fringe Dwellers*, Sydney, Pan Macmillan, 1966

Gedichtsammlungen:

- Oodgeroo Noonuccal: *My People*, Milton, The Jacaranda Press, 3rd ed. 1990
- *Inside Black Australia. An Anthology of Aboriginal Poetry*, ed. by Kevin Gilbert, Ringwood, Penguin Books Australia Ltd, 1988

Anthologie:

- *Paperbark. A collection of Black Australian writings*, ed. by Jack Davis, Stephen Muecke, Mudrooroo Narogin, Adam Shoemaker, St Lucia, University of Queensland Press, 1990

Teil II

Discover ... The Australian Aboriginals:
Das Schülerbuch im Unterricht

Das Schülerbuch im Unterricht

Vorbemerkungen zum Sprachgebrauch

Da sich der Sprachgebrauch ändert und das, was als politisch korrekt angesehen wird, vom Zeitgeist bestimmt ist, wandeln sich auch die Bezeichnungen, die die indigenen Australier vorzugsweise für sich verwenden.
Auf eine Anfrage des Verlages bezüglich des korrekten Titels für das vorliegende Themenheft antwortete FAIRA (Foundation for Aboriginal and Islander Research Action) im Dezember 1997: "When referring to the first inhabitants of Australia, prefer the forms Aboriginal (singular noun), Aboriginals (plural noun) and Aboriginal (adjective). While the form Aborigine is not acceptable as an alternative to Aboriginal for the singular noun, Aborigines may be used as an alternative plural form. These words should be dignified with a capital letter in the same way as Maori. Also in common usage by most groups are phrases such as Indigenous Peoples of Australia which is quite acceptable."
In dem Mitte 1998 erschienenen, von FAIRA herausgegebenen Sammelband *Bringing Australia Together,* hat sich der Sprachgebrauch bereits verändert. Während die Pluralform „Aboriginals" nicht mehr verwendet wird, bevorzugen die Autorinnen und Autoren die Begriffe „Indigenous people(s)", „Indigenous Australians", „Aboriginal people" und „Aborigines". In Analogie zu den beiden erstgenannten Begriffen werden die weißen Australier als „non-Indigenous Australians" bezeichnet.

Zu Bill Neidjie sei noch Folgendes angemerkt: Neidjie, ein „elder" der Gagudja people im heutigen Kakadu National Park, erzählt die Geschichte seines Volkes. Seine Worte muten wie Poesie an. Er möchte, dass sein Wissen erhalten bleibt und weitergereicht wird. Darum erzählt er seinen weißen Gesprächspartnern seine „story":

I give you this story.
This proper, true story.
People can listen.
I'm telling this while you've got time ...
time for you to make something,
you know ...
history ...
book.

(in: *Australia's Kakadu Man Bill Neidjie,* ed. by Bill Neidjie, Stephen Davis and Allan Fox, Darwin, Resource Managers Pty Ltd, 1986, p. 33)

Vorbemerkungen zur Einstiegsphase

Bei dem vorliegenden Thema erscheint es angebracht, den Kurs mit einer Einstiegsphase zu beginnen, in der die Schülerinnen und Schüler an den australischen Kontinent herangeführt werden, die die Beeinflussung des heutigen Sprachgebrauchs durch Wörter indigenen Ursprungs deutlich macht und in der sie bereits bekannte Begriffe wiederfinden, was wiederum den Zugang zum Thema erleichtern mag. Dazu eignet sich eine Overhead-Folie mit dem Arbeitsauftrag:

Do you know any of the following words? They all have something in common. Write down the meaning of the words you know and have a guess about the others.

Uluru
wombat
Woolloomooloo
koala
didgeridu
corroboree
Canberra
Kakadu
kangaroo
kookaburra
Kata Tjuta
boomerang
dingo
Nitmiluk

Answers:

All these words are derived from Aboriginal languages.

boomerang curved, flat, wooden missile
corroboree public performance of songs and dances of religious character
didgeridu a deep-toned wind instrument made from a hollow branch
Canberra Australian capital (supposed to mean "meeting place")
Woolloomooloo suburb of Sydney, New South Wales
Kakadu Kakadu National Park, Northern Territory. The name is derived from Ga:gudja or Gagadju, one of the languages of the region
Nitmiluk Katherine Gorge, Northern Territory
Uluru Ayers Rock (the world's largest monolith), about 400 km south-west of Alice Springs, Northern Territory
Kata Tjuta Mount Olga/The Olgas, near Uluru, meaning "Place of many heads"
(Seit der Rückgabe dieser Touristenattraktionen in den Besitz der jeweiligen indigenen Völker werden die englischen Bezeichnungen nur noch inoffiziell verwendet.)
dingo Australian wild dog
kangaroo, koala, wombat marsupials (*Beuteltiere*)
kookaburra bird with a cackling cry (laughing bird)

Bei der Erklärung der einzelnen Begriffe sollte es sich der Lehrer/die Lehrerin nicht nehmen lassen, diese durch Bilder zu veranschaulichen. Erst dann wird zum Beispiel klar, warum die Olgas

Place of many heads genannt werden. Informationsmaterial kann unter folgender Anschrift bestellt werden: Australian Tourist Commission, Neue Mainzer Strasse 22, 60311 Frankfurt/Main. Reiseprospekte können auch über Reisebüros bezogen werden.

Getting started

p. 5

Der Größenvergleich auf der „Getting started"-Seite soll den Schülerinnen und Schülern bewusst machen, welche Ausmaße der australische Kontinent einnimmt. Er erstreckt sich zwischen dem 10. und 45. Grad südlicher Breite und umfasst unterschiedliche Klimazonen. Das Vorurteil, dass es in Australien immer heiß ist, sollte also hier bereits ausgeräumt werden.

An dieser Stelle bietet es sich auch an, den Schülerinnen und Schülern minimale landeskundliche Kenntnisse zu vermitteln: Der *Commonwealth of Australia* besteht aus 6 Staaten (New South Wales, Victoria, Queensland, South Australia, Western Australia, Tasmania) und 2 Territorien (Australian Capital Territory, Northern Territory). Das Northern Territory bemüht sich seit einigen Jahren um seine „statehood", die mehr Unabhängigkeit gegenüber der Bundesregierung bedeutet. Dazu teilt die Australische Botschaft in ihrem *Lagebericht aus Australien* vom Oktober 1998 aber Folgendes mit: „Bei einer Volksabstimmung im Nordterritorium hat sich die Mehrheit der Wähler gegen eine Änderung des bisherigen Status des Territoriums ausgesprochen. Es wird damit vorerst nicht den Bundesstaaten voll gleichgestellt, sondern bleibt in einigen Aspekten im Zuständigkeitsbereich der australischen Bundesregierung."

Chapter 1: Life in Perfect Isolation – The Beginning

Vorbemerkungen zum Kapitel

Das vorliegende Themenheft ist chronologisch angeordnet. Texte aus späteren Kapiteln bauen auf Kenntnissen auf, die die Schülerinnen und Schüler in den Anfangskapiteln erworben haben. Es wäre daher ungünstig, diese zu überspringen. Sollte eine Kürzung des Stoffes aus Zeitgründen notwendig sein, so könnten die Kursteilnehmer/innen die einzelnen Texte oder Kapitel auf Referatbasis zusammenfassen und dem Kurs vortragen, damit die gewünschte Einheit erhalten bleibt.
Kapitel 1 enthält drei Grundlagentexte, die durch eine Karte und durch Bilder gestützt werden.
Die kleinen Übersichtskarten erscheinen immer dann, wenn in den Texten geografische Gegebenheiten genannt worden, die der Einordnung bedürfen. Dies geschieht mit Hilfe dieser Übersichtskarten.
Am Ende des Kapitels spricht Bill Neidjie „straight from the horse's mouth". Seine Worte unterstreichen die Bedeutung des Aboriginal „Law" und verleihen den Sachtexten größere Authentizität dadurch, dass die Schülerinnen und Schüler aus dem Munde eines „elder" erfahren, wie verbindlich die Gesetze aus der Schöpfungszeit heute noch sind.
Es empfiehlt sich, die Texte zu Hause vorbereiten zu lassen, damit das Kapitel in einer Doppelstunde durchgenommen werden kann.

Start here

Different ways of seeing the world around us p. 7

The original inhabitants of Australia lived in isolation from the rest of mankind for a very long time. It is therefore obvious that they had their own religious beliefs and world views.
What is your explanation for the natural phenomenon shown in this picture? What might it mean to the Aboriginal looking at it?

To the students it should be obvious that this "statue" is the work of erosion.
The Aboriginal, on the other hand, will see this as the work of the Great Spirits who have left their traces everywhere in the landscape.

The Arrival of the First Australians

Synopsis of the text

According to this text, the Aborigines have lived in Australia for about 40,000 years. They are supposed to have come from South-East Asia during the Pleistocene era, when the ocean was much lower than its present levels. At the end of the last Ice Age, the sea levels rose to those of today so that the original inhabitants of Australia lived in isolation from the rest of mankind.

Assignments

Activities

Thinking about the text p. 9 ➤

In what way do you think has this "effective isolation from the rest of mankind" shaped the country and its inhabitants?

This isolation has brought forward a flora and fauna (e.g. marsupials) that are unique to Australia. The first inhabitants represent a very old culture that did not mix much with people from other countries before the British invasion.

Hypothetical thinking p. 9 ➤

What might have been different if the sea levels had not risen but fallen?

Australia would have been accessible by land. There might have been invasions and wars. Australia might not be one single nation today.

The Creation Era

Synopsis of the text

According to Aboriginal belief, all life is part of an interconnected system that goes back to the Great Spirit Ancestors of the Dreamtime. The Ancestors are responsible for every aspect of Aboriginal people's lives. The Dreamtime continues as the *Dreaming* in the spiritual lives of Aboriginal people today.

Assignments

While-reading task

p. 10 ➤

What connection is there between *Dreamtime* and *Dreaming?*

Dreamtime means the Creation Era, but does not exclusively refer to the past. It is closely linked to the *Dreaming*, which keeps the dreamtime alive in spiritual ceremonies and has a strong impact on the Aborigines' lives.

Today, the two terms are defined differently: "Previously referred to as the Dreamtime, the term was changed to The Dreaming [...] in acknowledgement of the fact that the Aboriginal creative epoch cannot be understood within a Western framework of linear time. Western concepts of linear time with the separation of past and present make it difficult to describe The Dreaming as it is conceived in Aboriginal thought. While there is a sense in which The Dreaming activities occurred at the beginning of the world, and are past, there is a sense also in which they are still present. [...] The Aboriginal concept of time is therefore cyclic, rather than linear. [...] In an attempt to convey this idea, a scientist coined the term *everywhen*: The Dreaming was and is everywhen."

(*Aboriginal Australia*, ed. by Colin Bourke, Eleanor Bourke and Bill Edwards, St Lucia, University of Queensland Press, 1994, p. 67)

Activities

1. Say in your own words what this Creation Myth is about.

Understanding the text p. 10

According to Aboriginal belief, there is a basic link between the different forms of life, which all go back to the great Spirit Ancestors of the Dreamtime. They formed the features of the earth, gave the people the rules by which they were to live and which remain valid today. The Spirit Ancestors still control every aspect of nature, life and growth.

2. What do we learn about the importance of religion in the lives of Aboriginal people today?

The Aborigines seem to be deeply rooted in their religious beliefs, which form an important part of their daily lives.

The Desert Ancestors

Synopsis of the text

The beings of the Creation times formed the geography of the desert lands and provided food for the people living there. They established the law which is still followed by Aboriginal people today. The stories and legends of the Creation times are regarded as the absolute truth by Aboriginal people.

Assignments

Activities

How do Aboriginal people see the "beings of the Tjukurpa"?

Understanding the text p. 11

The beings of the Tjukurpa formed the shapeless earth into lands that could be inhabited. They also provided for the physical well-being of the inhabitants and gave them the *law* that is still followed by Aboriginal people today.

The stories and legends of the Creation times provided answers to the universal questions and problems throughout the ages. But did they prepare the Aboriginal peoples of Australia for the arrival of the Europeans who meant to take possession of the country?

Putting yourself in other people's position p. 11

The Europeans brought their own laws and expected the original inhabitants to abide by these laws. As they contained concepts that were utterly unknown to the Aborigines (e.g. the concept of private property), the Indigenous people stood no chance against the newcomers. Their lives were completely disrupted by the new laws.

Law Bill Neidjie

Author

Bill Neidjie was born in 1912 on the East Alligator River, which is today part of Kakadu National Park. He spent two years at a mission school, after which his mother took him to live in the bush. There he was fully initiated and became a rock and body painter.
During World War II, he worked for the military unit, maintaining a lighthouse. After the war he worked for 30 years as a cargo hand on a north coast lugger and acquired the nickname *Big Bill.* Tall and powerfully built, he could carry two large sacks of flour at a time, one on each shoulder.
In 1979, Neidjie returned to his home country. That year his people were awarded title to their land. They subsequently leased it to the federal government for inclusion in the Kakadu National Park, and Neidjie became a park ranger there.

Synopsis of the text

Unlike European law, which constantly changes at the politicians' will, Aboriginal law must be obeyed by everybody and cannot be changed.

Additional Text

The Beginning of Life Vivian Walker

Vivian Walker (1953-91), son of Oodgeroo Noonuccal, see students' book p. 33

For Aboriginal People, showing and telling other people is more important than writing instructions or books. If you were a young Aboriginal person you would hear many stories.
Vivian Walker, an Aboriginal writer, tells you this story of the Dreamtime. If you want to know what it is like to be a young Aboriginal, get someone to tell you the story.

Once, the sleeping earth was flat, dark and cold. No creature stirred. There were no hills and valleys, no trees or rivers.
In the centre of Australia, far beneath the surface of the earth, the Rainbow Serpent, Mother of Life, grew restless in her sleep. It was time for her to give birth to the children in her belly – all the animal tribes.
Slowly, she uncurled from her cramped sleeping place and began to burrow her way to the surface. But something stopped her. A great rock was in her way. For many many moons the Mother of Life pushed and pushed the boulder up. Inch by inch it moved until day, it burst on the surface. The Rainbow Serpent pushed it aside and looked around at the desolate landscape. She needed to rest from her labour. Before she set off on her wanderings, she turned to look at the rock which had gained its freedom like a baby, and she said: 'You are my first-born, you will be called Uluru.'
Her travels took her far and wide across the land. When she grew tired, she curled herself into a circle to sleep and regain her strength. When she awoke, she looked back and saw the deep winding tracks

where she had travelled. Where she had slept, great hollows had been left, looking out of place on the flat plains.

Now she felt the staggering pain of her babies crying to be free. It was time to return to Uluru. When she got back to the place of her first-born, she made herself ready. She called to the frog tribes inside her to come out. They had been sleeping for many many seasons and moved slowly, heavy with the water they had stored in their stomachs for the long hibernation before their birth. They shook their lazy heads. They did not want to give up their precious water but the wise mother tickled their stomachs. When they laughed, the water flowed in torrents from their mouths to fill the tracks of the Rainbow Serpent's wanderings, to make lakes and rivers, oceans and streams.

Suddenly, the scene was still. A far rumbling could be heard, and like a burst of laughter, grass began to grow, trees sprang up and flowers bloomed. Life had begun on earth. All the animal tribes, the kangaroo, the emu, the platypus and kookaburra flowed from the Rainbow Serpent to join their frog brothers. They flew and hopped, scurried and slithered all over the land and sky. They were happy on the earth.

platypus *Schnabeltier*

Now each animal stayed with his brothers and sisters, and hunted and played in harmony. The galah tribe preferred to live in the treetops and the snake tribe hunted between the rocks and trees. Each tribe knew that this was the law of the Rainbow Serpent.

galah [gəˈla] Australian bird: small cockatoo

The wise old woman looked at her happy children and said: 'There is food for all. Each tribe will be a totem. Let no one eat of his own totem for there is food for all. Those who keep this law, I will reward with human life. You and your children's children shall roam this land in happiness, hunting and playing forever. Those who disobey, I will punish and turn to stone, to sit in gloom until the end of time.'

And so it was. Those who broke the Rainbow Serpent's laws, she turned to mountains, hills and stones. They were left to sit while their brothers and sisters played and hunted at their feet. To those who kept the laws, she gave a human form and each human tribe kept as their totem the animal they had once been.

The tribes know themselves by their totems and a kangaroo man does not eat his brother, the kangaroo. In this way the Mother of Life, the Rainbow Serpent, makes sure that there is always food for all her children.

Chapter 2: The Arrival of the Pale-Skinned Strangers – The Invasion

Vorbemerkungen zum Kapitel

Kapitel 2 beginnt mit zwei Sachtexten, die über die britische Invasion informieren und erklären, wie die Briten ihr Vorgehen legitimierten. Die Bilder auf den Seiten 12 und 13 sollten dabei thematisiert werden, da sie die Textaussage ergänzen.
Der dritte Text ist sprachlich etwas schwieriger; die angegebenen Vokabelhilfen werden vermutlich nicht ausreichen. Hier könnte ein Schüler/eine Schülerin die Aufgabe übernehmen eine zusätzliche Liste mit Erklärungen zu erstellen, die dem Kurs vor Durchnahme des Textes zur Verfügung gestellt wird.
Das Gedicht sollte möglichst laut (und emphatisch) vorgetragen werden. Wenn der Kurslehrer/die Kurslehrerin nicht zu solchen Vorstellungen neigt, u.a. weil ihm/ihr dies zu distanzlos erscheint, könnte er/sie den Text auf Band sprechen (oder sprechen lassen) und dem Kurs vorspielen.
Die Worte Bill Neidjies hingegen eignen sich weniger zum lauten Vortrag, da sie das *non-standard English* des Sprechers wiedergeben.
Das Kapitel endet mit der Ausweitung des Blickwinkels auf ein weiteres indigenes Volk, die nordamerikanischen Indianer. Es bietet sich an, dass die Kursteilnehmerinnen und Kursteilnehmer zusätzliche Informationen über deren Weltsicht sammeln, damit sie zu einem Kulturvergleich befähigt werden.

Start here

Speculating about the original inhabitants **p. 12**

This is how an Aboriginal child sees the arrival of the first British ship in Australia.
Before you go on reading, try to imagine how the arrival of the Europeans changed the Aboriginal peoples' lives.

One can easily imagine how every aspect of the Aboriginal peoples' lives changed. The first settlers came from a country in which the Industrial Revolution was well on its way. The convicts had fallen victim to a system in which private property was highly valued. In fact, most of them had been convicted and exiled for minor theft. When they came to Australia, they found that its inhabitants lived like stone-age people, were hunters and gatherers, for whom sharing and socializing represented higher values than the possession of goods. Consequently they looked down on them and even the lowliest of the convicts felt superior to the Indigenous inhabitants of Australia.

The Invaders

Synopsis of the text

In 1788, thirteen ships arrived in Botany Bay: the British fleet of eleven ships under the command of Captain Arthur Phillip, and two French ships. Captain Phillip must have been shocked at the sight of the French ships, but he need not have worried as they sailed off into the Pacific two months later, and were never heard from again. The pictures on this page are examples of the Indigenous peoples' reactions to the first sightings of white men wearing hats and riding horses.
The last paragraph of the text hints at the hard times to come for the Indigenous Australians.

Assignments

While-reading tasks

p. 13

What difference is there between this invasion and the Aboriginals' first encounter with Cook?

Cook's party was a small one and left after having explored the coastal region.
The arrival of so many ships, however, must have completely overwhelmed and scared the original inhabitants. Everything about the invaders was strange: their outward appearance, their behaviour, their clumsiness in the bush. But the realization that these strangers obviously meant to stay must have caused the greatest shock to the original inhabitants.

p. 14

Explain the metaphorical language.

The figurative language shows how the little settlement that started on the east coast of the country grew in size and spread over the whole continent, bringing destruction and death to many inhabitants.

Activities

Getting the facts right p. 14

Describe the arrival of the first ships in your own words.

Eighteen years after the discovery of the east coast of Australia by Captain James Cook in 1770, the first fleet of eleven ships under the command of Captain Arthur Phillip arrived in Botany Bay. In addition to the British ships, two French ships on their voyage of exploration dropped anchor in Botany Bay. Masses of people got off the British ships, among them 700 convicts who had been kept under deck and therefore were in pitiful condition.

Empathizing with other people
p. 14

Can you imagine the Aboriginals' feelings when they first saw the masses of strange white people coming to their shores? On the other hand, can you imagine what it must have been like for the convicts to have been forcibly sent to that unknown continent? Who would you feel more sorry for?

The Aborigines must have been torn between feelings of surprise, curiosity, fear, and possibly also amusement: "These trembling savages seemed quite astonished at the figure we cut in being clothed. I think it is very easy to conceive the ridiculous figure we must appear to these poor creatures, who were perfectly naked."
(*The Fatal Shore* by Robert Hughes, London, Pan Books Ltd, 1988, p. 84)

The convicts were exiles and their punishment made them belong to the lowest of the low. It must have been a terrible fate for them to have been sent to this unknown continent, 15,000 miles away from home, with little hope of returning to their families. Today this seems harsh punishment, considering that in many cases their "crimes" were caused by poverty and neglect.

Projects: Collecting information about other historical events
p. 14

Split up into groups and work on one of the following projects:

1. The arrival of the First Fleet in Australia in 1788 cannot be seen as an isolated historical event. It is important to know what was happening in other parts of the world at that time. Find out what the political and economic situation was like in
   - Great Britain
   - North America
   - France.

   What important events were taking place in those countries at roughly the same time?

Great Britain: Industrial Revolution. In 1760, great mechanical inventions began to revolutionize production and society in England, replacing rural domestic industries by the factory system in industrial cities of Northern England.

North America: War of Independence from 1775-81. The British were no longer able to get cheap raw materials from America and to ship their convicts to the New World. Consequently, they were interested in finding new colonies.

France: French Revolution in 1789.

Terra Nullius

Synopsis of the text

This text explains the concept of *terra nullius*, a Latin term meaning "no-man's-land", which provided the basis for the appropriation of the Australian continent by the British government in the name of the Crown.

Assignments

Activities

1. Explain the concept of *Terra Nullius*.

Terra Nullius is a legal doctrine referring to land that does not belong to anyone and can therefore be brought under control and owned by those claiming it.

Understanding the doctrine of *Terra Nullius* p. 15

2. Why did the British government think that there was a legal basis for the appropriation of the Australian continent?

The British thought that the legal doctrine of *Terra Nullius* applied to the Australian continent. They believed that they were peacefully occupying a country inhabited by people who had no settled laws or customs and who did not make proper use of the land (according to European standards).

3. Why did Cook and Banks hold to the doctrine of *Terra Nullius* even when they found the country inhabited?

Cook and Banks were of the opinion that the original inhabitants were not "civilized" enough to own the country. As nomadic hunter-gatherers, they did not live according to the Europeans' ideas of land-ownership, which included fixed habitations and the cultivation of the land.

4. Aboriginal people call it "invasion" while the British speak of "peaceful occupation" or "peaceful settlement". Who is right in your opinion?

To answer this question, the students must try to empathize with two very different interest groups. The course might split up into settlers and original inhabitants who take up the issue from their opposing positions.

According to Aboriginal law, people cannot own land (or animals or plants etc.) but they are rather owned by the land, they are part of it. This belief stood in contradiction to the newcomers' idea of ownership. They judged the unknown land and its inhabitants according to their own European standards, which included a marked sense of ownership.

Conflicting concepts p. 16

Would it have been possible for the first settlers to understand the Aboriginals' spirituality and its implications for their everyday life? Do you think they tried to do this?

As the following text shows, it must have been extremely difficult for the first white Australians to understand the Indigenous peoples. Even if they had tried to, their preconceived ideas about religion and their different value systems would have prevented them from doing so.

First Encounters – Value Clashes

Robert Hughes

Synopsis of the text

This text is an excerpt from Robert Hughes, *The Fatal shore, A History of the Transportation of Convicts to Australia 1787-1868.* It deals with the first encounters of the Europeans with the original inhabitants of Australia. The situation must seem ironic to us: The convicts, most of whom had committed crimes against property, were taken to a land where private property was unknown. In another part of the book the author tells us that the Aborigines left their tools and weapons lying in the open. So the convicts stole them and sold them as souvenirs to be taken back to England.

Assignments

While-reading tasks

p. 16

Why did the Aboriginals display "such a marked sense of territory"?

The following text excerpts further elucidate the topic: "Aboriginal culture cannot be separated from the land. On the land are stories – Aboriginal stories that explain why people, rockholes, the hills and the trees came to be there. The land is full of stories. Every square mile is just like a book, a book with a lot of pages, and it's all a story for the children to learn."

(*Aboriginal Australia,* ed. by Colin Bourke, Eleanor Bourke and Bill Edwards, St Lucia, University of Queensland Press, 1994, p. 45)

"The land, my mother. Like a human mother, the land gives us protection, enjoyment, and provides for our needs: economic, social and religious. We have a human relationship with the land: mother, daughter, son. When the land is taken from us or destroyed, we feel hurt because we belong to the land, and we are a part of it."

("Needs and Means of Combating Racism" by Andrew Theophanous, in: *Bringing Australia Together. The Structure and Experience of Racism in Australia,* published by The Foundation for Aboriginal and Islander Research Action, Woolloongabba, 1998, p. 101)

p. 17

Why were the Whites of the opinion that the Aboriginals had no religious beliefs?

"The early European observers of Aboriginal life came with preconceived ideas about what religion and spiritual existence represented, based on their experience in Western Europe of Christianity, church buildings, forms of worship, the roles of priests and ministers, belief in one God and the importance of scriptures. When they observed similar phenomena of rites, holy men, shrines or temples and sacred books in Africa and Asia they acknowledged the presence of religious systems. However, as the forms of religious expression in Australia were so different and subtle, their very existence was denied."

(*Aboriginal Australia*, ed. by Colin Bourke, Eleanor Bourke and Bill Edwards, St Lucia, University of Queensland Press, 1994, p. 66)

How does Hunter's language reveal his feelings about the first Australians?

p. 17

The word "animal" used in connection with the first inhabitants shows Hunter's attitude towards them.

Activities

Check your list and try to find reasons why most of the things mentioned in the first paragraph must have been absolutely incomprehensible to the convicts.

Explaining the text/ evaluating the facts p. 17

None of the things important to Georgian culture could be found in Australia. How were the convicts to understand that the Indigenous Australians had "no property, no money ..." when they were exiled for having stolen a ration of food?

1. Why is the Aboriginal concept of religion so difficult to grasp for people brought up within our Western culture? Does the term *religion* apply at all?

Comparing different cultures p. 17

The answer to this question is given in the last part of the text: "they carried their conception of the sacred, of mythic time and ancestral origins with them as they walked." (ll. 34-36) So there were no visible signs of a developed religion.

2. Speaking in Western terms, which of the two cultures seems to be more deeply rooted in religion?

The term *religion* is part of our Western culture and not really applicable to the Aborigines' spirituality.
The following *Spiritual Song of the Aborigine* gives an impressive example of what spirituality means to Aboriginal people.

Spiritual Song of the Aborigine

Hyllus Maris

Author

Hyllus Maris (1934-86) was born, lived and worked in the state of Victoria. A sociologist and well-known Aboriginal activist, she founded the first Aboriginal school in that state. In addition to writing poems and short stories, she collaborated with the Austrian-born author, Sonia Borg, on the film script and the novel entitled *Women of the Sun* (1982), a history of Australia over the previous 200 years, as seen through the experiences of a number of Aboriginal women.

Synopsis of the text

According to Aboriginal belief, people cannot own land or plants or animals, but they are rather owned by the land, they are part of it. This is what is expressed in this poem. The speaker is not only part of nature but also of the Dreamtime, which makes him/her belong to the past as well as to the present.

Assignments

While-reading tasks

p. 18 ➤

Who is the speaker?

The speaker is an Aboriginal person who tells the readers what being Aboriginal means to her/him.

p. 18 ➤

What is your first reaction to this poem?

The students might be surprised at the self-assured way in which the Aboriginal speaker defines her/his place in the spiritual and natural world. From a Christian point of view such a way of seeing oneself would not only be presumptious but almost blasphemous.

Activities

Comparing different ideas about spirituality p. 18

1. What is the basic difference between this concept and that of Christianity?

While Christians must strive and struggle to deserve their entrance into paradise, to eventually "share the spiritual essence", "Aboriginal people derive their spiritual essence from the Ancestral Spirit Beings and share the same spiritual essence which inhabits the land and other species."

2. Some people in our society claim to be indifferent to religious matters or to be agnostics or atheists. Would it be possible for an Aboriginal to hold a similar view?

A religion that people choose to practice or not to practice is unconceivable to Aboriginal thinking.

The Vengeance of the Spirit Ancestors

Synopsis of the text

Aboriginal people believe that the Great Ancestors are very angry at the white intruders' disrespectful behaviour concerning sacred sites. Aboriginal law demands that these places be respected. Therefore, the Spirit Ancestors send diseases, floods and destructive storms, such as Cyclone Tracy, to show their anger and to take revenge.

Assignments

While-reading tasks

In what way have sacred sites been desecrated?

p. 19

As the newcomers were not familiar with Aboriginal law, they intruded on sacred sites or took shelter in sacred caves without knowing that they were offending the Great Ancestors.

Why do the mining companies in particular arouse the wrath of the Great Ancestors?

p. 19

The mining companies' offences are more serious since they actually remove the earth, thus not only disturbing nature's harmony, but also interfering with the landscape that was shaped by the Great Ancestors.

Why is Jambuwal angry and with whom?

p. 19

Jambuwal, the Thunder Man, is angry at the Whites and at the mining companies because he holds them responsible for the destruction of sacred sites. Jambuwal does not seem to like the idea of black people being put into white prisons, either.

What is the Whites' reaction to the conflicts they cause in some Aboriginals' minds?

p. 19

They do not really seem to try to understand the importance of sacred sites for Aboriginal people. In this case, the Aboriginal bulldozer operator was imprisoned and left to die. He was one of the numerous *deaths in custody* (see student's book, p. 47).

Activities

1. How do you judge the incident in Halls Creek?
2. Who is responsible for the Aboriginal man's death?

Discussing differing world views/conflicting situations p. 20

The students should discuss the incident and try to understand what motivated the behaviour of both parties. They are not supposed to find concrete answers to the second question, but to evaluate the situation from different points of view.

(How) can conflicts of this kind be solved?

Finding solutions p. 20

The same goes for this question. If the answer was an easy one, it would probably have been found by now. The teacher should rather encourage the students to discuss what causes conflicts of this kind and to make suggestions for possible solutions.
The following extract from *The Aboriginal Children's History of Australia* might add different aspects to the discussion: "Wuyal was the wild honey spirit. He made the mountain at Nhulunbuy[1] and everywhere he went he left sugarbag[2] for the people. The mining people

put a water tank on Wuyal's mountain. Our people were very sad and angry.
Before the mining there were animals everywhere and it was a pretty place. Now it's ruined. We've only got a few animals, and there are lots of beer cans and smoke and grog[3] and it's dusty everywhere around Melville Bay. There is a special banyan tree[4] called Dhanburama, right in the middle of the alumina plant. The mining men must not touch the sacred tree because it has the spirit of Wuyal in it. There was a big argument about the sacred tree. There was a big argument about the land. Now white people have to pay royalty money to build houses and the town at Nhulunbuy and to take out the bauxite."

(*The Aboriginal Children's History of Australia,* written and illustrated by Australia's Aboriginal Children, Rigby Limited, Adelaide, Sydney, Melbourne, Perth, Brisbane: Aboriginal Arts Board, Australia Council, 1977, p. 93)

[1] **Nhulunbuy** town on the Gove Peninsula at the north-east tip of Arnhem Land (NT) – [2] **sugerbag** wild honey – [3] **grog** (inf) alcohol – [4] **banyan tree** fig tree, whose branches send out roots to the ground, sometimes causing the tree to spread over a wide area

Land Bill Neidjie

Synopsis of the text

Bill Neidjie explains in his own words that the law must be respected by Indigenous as well as non-Indigenous Australians. The desecration of sacred sites will be punished.

Big Bill Neidjie

Synopsis of the text

In this short text the words of Bill Neidjie and those of Chief Seattle are compared. Both address the white people with an appeal for the earth.

Assignments

Activities

Project: comparing similar cultures p. 21

Find out more about the American Indians' world view, their religious beliefs, and compare your findings to the Australian Indigenous peoples' way of seeing the world around them.

Then you might have a discussion in your course comparing the Indigenous peoples' concepts with our Western culture and finally evaluate them in terms of their respect for nature.

Comparing different cultures p. 21

The texts quoted in the student's book show that there are similarities between these two Indigenous peoples. The students should collect more information for a better understanding of both cultures so that they are able to compare them with our Western culture.

Chapter 3: "They Were Not Fit to Live within the General Community" – From Protection to Assimilation

Vorbemerkungen zum Kapitel

Während der erste Text von Kapitel 3 über „Protection" informiert, macht das Kurzdrama die Auswirkungen der „Protection Laws" auf den einzelnen Menschen deutlich. Die Darstellung des Einzelschicksals im fiktionalen Text sollte den Schülerinnen und Schülern den affektiven Zugang zur Problematik ermöglichen und ihre Identifikationsbereitschaft auslösen. Das Drama sollte mit verteilten Rollen gelesen werden, möglichst von Schülerinnen und Schülern die sich nicht scheuen ihre Rolle emotional vorzutragen.

Die beiden nächsten Texte ergänzen sich thematisch und sollten zusammen behandelt werden. Das Gedicht führt in das Thema *ethnocentrism* ein und bereitet auf die im folgenden Text vorgestellte Assimilationsidee vor. Die Realisierung dieser Idee und ihre Auswirkungen auf die Betroffenen ist Gegenstand des Cartoons und der beiden folgenden literarischen Texte. Das Klagelied, mit Empathie vorgetragen, löst Betroffenheit aus dadurch, dass es das im vorangehenden Sachtext dargestellte Thema der Assimilationspolitik jetzt am Beispiel einer „verwaisten" Mutter wieder aufgreift.

Der Romanauszug hat ebenfalls das Thema *stolen generation* zum Inhalt, jedoch aus der Perspektive des „gestohlenen" Kindes. Obwohl von gleicher Tragik, wirkt dieser Text aufgrund des ironischen Stils eher erheiternd. Um dies deutlich zu machen, bietet es sich an, ihn laut zu lesen und die Rolle des „Sherman priest" mit übertrieben deutschem Akzent zu sprechen. Die Absurdität der Situation dürfte so besonders deutlich werden.

Das abschließende Gedicht mit dem Titel *Integration* gibt eine Antwort darauf, was die Aborigines anstelle von Assimilation wünschen. Es leitet zur Thematik von Kapitel 4 über.

Start here

Living by different laws p. 22

How do you think the Aboriginals managed to live by three different laws?

From what the students have learned by now about the importance of Aboriginal traditional law, they should be able to fully appreciate the disruptive impact of such confusing, contradictory and humiliating laws on the Indigenous people's lives. The substitution of Aboriginal law by European law further meant the breaking down of the old system by which the original inhabitants had lived for over 40,000 years.

Protectors of Aborigines

Synopsis of the text

"Protection" of Aboriginal people originally meant converting them to Christianity, defending them against white settlers, educating their children and supervising them until they were considered fit to live within the general community. In time, however, the Aborigines Protection Board gained absolute control over the daily lives of Aboriginal people.

Assignments

Activities

1. What was the original aim of protection?

Gaining an insight into the aim of protection p. 23

The British wanted
- to convert the Aborigines to Christianity
- to protect them against offenders/intruders
- to educate them
- to provide special laws for them until they were seen fit to live within the wider community.

2. How did this aim change in the course of time?

What started as *protection* gradually became control and paternalism so that Aboriginal people no longer felt protected but persecuted by the people whose task it was to protect them.

The Girl Who Was Taken Away from Her Family

Selma Sampson Nampijinpa

Synopsis of the text

Scene 1: Violet, a part-Aboriginal girl, lives with her family in a reserve. A white couple have come to take her away and make her work for them as a domestic servant, despite Violet and her mother's protests.

Scene 2: Violet works very hard in the big house. She is unhappy and misses her family. The couple's son, John, feels sorry for her and helps her to escape by taking her back to the reserve in his parents' car.

Scene 3: Violet's family and friends are happy to see her back. John tells them that he does not like his parents either, and expresses his wish to stay in the reserve. Violet will teach him the Aboriginal way of life. To celebrate this happy event the mother and the girls dance around the campfire while John and the men look on.

Assignments

While-reading tasks

p. 24 ➤ Watch out for a protector to help Violet.

The students will notice that there is no protector. Neither Violet nor her mother think of calling the protector as this would be a futile undertaking.

p. 24 ➤ Why must Violet go with the white couple?

Since there is no protection for Aboriginal people, there is nothing the mother could do to stop the white couple from taking her daughter away.

p. 24 ➤ Who is John?

John obviously belongs to the white family.

p. 25 ➤ What kind of people are Mr and Mrs Woods?

They are selfish, unfriendly, racist people who think that the Blacks must serve them.

p. 25 ➤ What do you think of John's decision?

John's decision does not come as a real surprise after what he has already done. His reaction is humane, though rather unlikely.

p. 25 ➤ Is it a happy ending?

For the moment, everybody around Violet is happy. But the happiness will not last, since Mr and Mrs Woods will surely come to take back their son, Violet and the car.

Activities

Understanding the play p. 25 ➤ The play opens with Violet crying and ends with Violet dancing. What happens in between to cause this change?

With the white boy John's help, Violet has resisted the white people. This is a moment of victory for her and her family.

Evaluating the play p. 25 ➤ Is John a realistic character? What role does he play?

John is a character that results from the author's wishful thinking and is therefore not realistic. He takes on the role of Violet's protector while official protection does not exist.

Writing option p. 25 ➤ The author has chosen a very optimistic but rather unlikely ending for her play. Rewrite scene three based on your knowledge of Aboriginal life under Protection Laws.

In a more realistic version, the police would arrive at the reserve even before Violet and John in order to take them back to the Woods' place.

"Oh Don't You Wish that You Were Me"

This children's verse exemplifies what *ethnocentrism* means. The child speaker feels sorry for the children who must live overseas and therefore cannot be "safe" and "live at home".

Synopsis of the text

Assignments

Activities

1. What examples of *strangeness* does the speaker (an English child) give?

Close-up of words and contents p. 26

"Scarlet trees", "lions", "ostriches" and "turtles" are not found in Britain, but have no negative connotations. On the contrary, at the beginning of the poem the examples sound interesting, even exciting.

2. To what conclusion does the speaker come? (lines 9-16)

The speaker comes to the conclusion that, however nice life overseas might be, it cannot be as nice as that of the children living in England for the simple reason that the children addressed in this poem do not live in England.

Why should the children addressed in this poem wish they were British?

Applying the definition of ethnocentrism p. 26

The speaker holds the view that only the British way of life guarantees real happiness.

"Love White Men and Learn to Speak English"

This article from *The Encyclopaedia of Aboriginal Australia* outlines the policy of *assimilation*. The words used by the governor in his address to South Australian Aboriginals are strikingly similar to the ideas expressed in the poem.

Synopsis of the text

Assignments

Activities

Comparing and evaluating other people's opinions p. 27

1. Compare the ideas expressed by the child speaker of the poem with the governor's opinion.

Basically, the governor expresses the same opinion as the child speaker with the difference that he is more straightforward and explicit.

2. What basic misconception underlies both?

They both believe that there is no other way to happiness but the white people's way.

Defining the term *civilization* p. 27

1. In the eyes of Australia's colonial administrators, the Aboriginals were 'uncivilized'. Would you share this opinion?

The first question should be answered spontaneously and affectively by the students. Their first reactions might be quite revealing as far as cultural clichés are concerned.

2. Try to define the term 'civilization' and give examples of 'civilized' or 'uncivilized' behaviour.

The second task demands a cognitive approach. The students might find definitions that stand in opposition to the answers given before. Some might even come to a new understanding of civilization.

"This Is Your Lucky Day ..."

Assignments

Activities

Understanding the aim of the cartoonist p. 28

1. What point does the cartoonist, Geoff Pryor, want to make?

The cartoonist wants to show that the practice of forced assimilation represented a violation of human rights.

2. Is he successful in your opinion?

The cartoonist points to the cruelties of assimilation by shocking the readers with a cruel picture. He shows in a condensed form how the Indigenous Australians were deprived of their Aboriginal identity (e.g. the young man is addressed with a Christian name).

Some students might find that the woman resembles Mrs Thatcher and that the car reminds them of the RSPCA (Royal Society for the Prevention of Cruelty to Animals) collecting stray animals. These associations intensify the point made by the cartoonist.

3. This cartoon appeared in a Canberra newspaper. How would you as a reader have reacted to it? Do you think it shocked a lot of people? Is that what the cartoonist wanted?

The cartoon must have touched the readers' feelings. Some will have protested to the newspaper. The cartoonist obviously wanted to provoke such reactions and start a new discussion on this subject.

Brown Skin Baby Bob Randall

Author

Bob (Robert) Randall was born in 1934 near Uluru (Ayers Rock). As a child he was taken from his parents and sent to an orphanage in Arnhem Land. He became a social welfare worker and later receivod a diploma in the area of special education. As well as being a prose writer, Randall writes songs about the suffering of Aboriginal people during white settlement.

Synopsis of the text

One day, while riding through the countryside, a missionary meets a young black mother. She is crying and grieving for her baby that was taken away by force. She tells him how the police came to take her part-Aboriginal baby to an orphanage where he is made to lose his Aboriginal identity.

Assignments

While-reading task

p. 29

What is your first impression? Do you sympathize with the black mother?

Like the cartoon, the poem deals with the policy of assimilation. There is a shift of perspective to a young black mother whose baby has been taken away. Her deeply felt sorrow touches the reader.

Activities

Getting the message of the poem p. 29

1. Why does the young black mother put so much emphasis on the baby's skin colour?

"From white man boss that baby I have" (line 11) is her explanation. The baby is a "half-caste" (see page 27) and must not be raised by his mother, since he is considered suitable for assimilation.

2. What does the fact that the baby's father is his mother's white boss tell us about the relationship between the white property owners and their black women servants?

The white boss most probably took his black servant by force and is not likely to own the baby.

3. Do you think the father could have prevented or wanted to prevent the police from taking the baby away? What role might he play?

Obviously, the white boss takes no interest in the child he has fathered. So there is no-one to help the young black mother.

4. Explain lines 21 to 22.

The child experiences a second uprooting when he has to leave the mission which has become his home. As the children were sent away to work on farms or to be domestic workers at a rather early age, this second uprooting must have been very painful for them.

Wandering Girl – Unna You Fullas

Glenyse Ward

Author

Glenyse Ward was born in Perth, WA, in 1949. When she was one year old, she was taken from her parents to be put into an orphanage. At the age of three, a German Catholic priest took her to a mission run by Germans. She now lives in Broome, northwest Australia, and is working on a new book.

Synopsis of the text

In the first excerpt the author tells us that she was taken from her natural parents and put into an orphanage when she was very small. At the age of three she was taken to another orphanage run by German Catholic missionaries. She recalls the strange looks and behaviour of the missionaries and her strict up-bringing there.

In the second excerpt, the priest who has been in charge of the mission is celebrating his last mass before going home to "Shermany" to retire. In his last sermon he speaks of the love and dedication that the brothers, nuns and priests have given to the children and reminds them not to forget what they have been taught, in order to make the white people they will work for happy.

Assignments

While-reading tasks

p. 30 ➤

How does the narrator assess the practice of institutionalizing part Aboriginal children?

According to the author, the most crucial consequences for the *stolen* children were estrangement from their families and loss of identity.

p. 30 ➤

Imagine how this repeated uprooting might have affected the baby.

There was no stability in the baby's life. As soon as she started to settle down, she was taken to another mission. She must have lacked the security a child needs.

What were "these things"?

◀ p. 30

The missionaries wore glasses. The black children had not seen glasses before.

Does this mistake sound familiar to you?

◀ p. 30

The students will recall the early stages of their struggle with the English language, when they might have "become" a letter from their grandmother.

What is different today?

◀ p. 31

The priest seems to be very sad about leaving the mission.

Describe the priest's emotional state.

◀ p. 31

The priest has lost his self-assurance and falls prey to his emotions.

What attitude towards the mission children does he display?

◀ p. 31

He expresses his love for the mission children, to whom he has dedicated his entire life.

What seems to be the aim of his work in the mission?

◀ p. 31

He is quite explicit about the aim: to produce strong farm workers and domestic cleaners who will make the white people they work for very happy.

Why is this such a sad moment for Glenyse?

◀ p. 31

After all, the mission has become Glenyse's home, and the departure of the father in charge is comparable to losing, if not a real father, a person who was near to her and who led her through part of her life.

Activity

It is now up to you to judge the benefits of the practice of institutionalizing part Aboriginal children.

◀ Forming your own opinion p. 31

This text provides some controversial material for discussion. To the course, the fact that this is a German mission and the children are forced to abide by German/Catholic rules might be of particular interest.

Link-Up Wants to Help

Synopsis of the text

This text is taken from a brochure addressed to Aboriginal people who were separated from their families when they were children and to Aboriginal families who want to find their children who were taken away. *Link-Up* is an Aboriginal organization that offers to help these people cope with their problems.

Assignments

Activities

Understanding the aims and the necessity of *Link-Up* p. 32

1. What are the reasons for the foundation of such an organization?

The organization wants to help Aboriginal people who were separated from their families when they were children, but also Aboriginal families whose children were taken away.

2. How do they want to help?

They offer practical help by accompanying Aboriginal people who are going to meet their families for the first time.

3. What kind of problems might people who were forcefully separated from their families when they were children have today?

They might have been estranged from the Aboriginal life-style since they were "forced to abide by the European way" (see page 30, lines 5-6). They might no longer speak their native language and thus be unable to communicate with their families. They might even feel ashamed of their parents and families living in the bush, if their Europeanization has been very "successful". They might need professional help, such as a therapy etc.

Assimilation – No! Integration – Yes! Oodgeroo Noonuccal

Author

Oodgeroo Noonuccal (1920-93), formerly Kath Walker, was born on Stradbroke Island, Queensland, of the Noonuccal people. At the age of sixteen, she applied for training as a nurse but was rejected because she was Aboriginal. During World War II, she spent four years in the Australian Women's Army Service. In the 1960s, she became politically active and also started writing poetry, short stories, essays, speeches and plays. In 1970, she was awarded an MBE (Member of the Order of the British Empire) for services to the community. However, she returned it in 1987 as a protest against the forthcoming Australian Bicentenary celebrations.

Synopsis of the text

In the first two lines of the first poem, Oodgeroo Noonuccal expresses her opinion about assimilation: it annihilates the weaker part.
In the second poem she advocates integration. The poem ends with an appeal that "black and white may go forward together in harmony and brotherhood".

Assignments

Activities

Poems against oppression? p. 33

1. What is Oodgeroo Noonuccal's opinion about assimilation?

Oodgeroo Noonuccal thinks that assimilation means absorbing the Aborigines into white society with the ultimate effect of destroying their culture.

2. Comment on the speaker's attitude in the first part of the second poem.

The speaker seems to be grateful to the Whites, the advanced race, for having taught them how to live properly. But lines 7 to 9 reveal the author's irony.

3. Where does this attitude change?

The attitude changes in line 10 when the speaker begins to differentiate between the things they had to give up, "the price of survival", and the things they want to keep.

4. What is the speaker's conclusion?

The poem culminates in the rhetorical question: "Why change our sacred myths for your sacred myths?" (line 18). The speaker concludes that Aboriginal people do not want assimilation but integration.

5. Oodgeroo Noonuccal said that her poems were pure propaganda. How do you judge the effectiveness of this kind of political activity?

The students should think of any political poems they know and exchange their ideas about their estimated effectiveness.

Complete text of the poem:

Assimilation – No!

Pour your pitcher of wine into the wide river
And where is your wine? There is only the river.
Must the genius of an old race die
That the race might live?
We who would be one with you, one people,
We must surrender now much that we love,
The old freedoms for new musts,
Your world for ours,
But a core is left that we must keep always.
Change and compel, slash us into shape,
But not our roots deep in the soil of old.
We are different hearts and minds
In a different body. Do not ask of us
To be deserters, to disown our mother,
To change the unchangeable.
The gum cannot be trained into an oak.

Something is gone, something surrendered, still
We will go forward and learn.
Not swamped and lost, watered away, but keeping
Our own identity, our pride of race.
Pour your pitcher of wine into the wide river
And where is your wine? There is only the river.

(in: *My People* by Oodgeroo Noonuccal, Milton, The Jacaranda Press, 3rd ed., 1990, p. 21)

Chapter 4: "Aboriginals Are a People, Not a Minority" – On the Way to Self-Management

Vorbemerkungen zum Kapitel

Abgesehen von dem Exzerpt aus *The Fringe Dwellers*, der mit ca. 1100 Wörtern zu den längeren Texten dieses Themenheftes gehört, setzt sich Kapitel 4 aus mehreren kurzen Texten zusammen, die inhaltlich verzahnt sind.
Die Anfangstexte schildern einige Etappen auf dem Weg zur Selbstverwaltung und können zügig durchgearbeitet werden.
Den Schwerpunkt des Kapitels bildet der zweite Teil (ab Seite 39). Es geht um die Diskussion von Grundfragen, die in den Ausgangstexten (Zeitungsartikel, Kolumne, Leserbrief, Romanauszug) unterschiedliche Bewertung finden. Die Kursteilnehmer/innen sind aufgefordert, sich an der durch die unterschiedlichen Texte ausgelösten Diskussion zu beteiligen und ihr persönliches Meinungsbild zu entwickeln. Als schriftliche Übungsform bietet sich hierbei das Verfassen von Leserbriefen an.

Start here

The Aboriginal flag – a symbol of unity p. 34

What function may the flag have had on the Aboriginals' way to self-management?

It must be kept in mind that the Indigenous Australians had no common language and that they were not a homogenous people. At the time of the British invasion, there were over 250 language groups speaking up to 600 dialects. These groups were not always on friendly terms. In the 1970s, it was still difficult to bring so many different peoples together.
The flag had to symbolize something all the Indigenous peoples had in common and that could be understood by everybody. The colours Harold Thomas chose for the flag represent the basic features with which all Aboriginal people can identify: the black colour of their skin, the red mother earth and the yellow sun as the giver of life. The flag has become a strong symbol of Aboriginal unity.

From Protection to Self-Management

Synopsis of the text

Four broad phases may be distinguished in the policy on Aboriginal and Torres Strait Islander administration: protection, assimilation, integration, and self-management.

Assignments

Activities

Identifying the four phases **p. 35**

1. Establish a timeline of the four phases and say what the chief aim of each phase was/is.

Four phases

I. 1788 – 1930s and 40s: protection
aim: protection of Aboriginal people

II. 1930s – 1970: assimilation
two different aims:
– raising Indigenous people to the same levels of education, health and material comforts as white Australians
– absorbing Indigenous people into the wider society through cultural change and intermarriage

III. late 1960s onwards: integration leading to self-determination
two different aims:
– attainment of the living standards achieved by non-Indigenous Australians
– maintenance of a distinct cultural identity

IV. mid 1970s – present: self-management
aim: creation of self-managing Indigenous institutions and organizations

2. Then describe the development that has taken place.

Since 1788, the Indigenous Australians have gradually made their way from being controlled by the non-Indigenous Australians to self-determination.

The Torres Strait Islanders and Their New Flag

Synopsis of the text

The Torres Strait Islanders used to be grouped with Aboriginal people, but they have their own distinctive culture, traditions and history. Only recently have they achieved official recognition. Like the Aborigines, they wanted a flag as a symbol of their unity. After its design was agreed upon, it was given equal prominence with the Aboriginal flag.

Love and Marriage

Synopsis of the text

The writer of this letter to the editor expresses her personal view: she suggests that the Union Jack be removed from the Australian flag and that the Aboriginal flag take its place.

Assignments

Activities

Does the last sentence come as a surprise to you? Discuss Ms Foxwell's suggestion.

Changing the flag
p. 38

Ms Foxwell expresses her personal opinion, which is not representative.
About one half of the Australians are republicans, which means that they would like to see Australia as a republic with a president as head of state. They might be willing to consider this idea. The other half would like to leave things as they are, with Queen Elizabeth as head of state, represented in Australia by the governor-general. These people would not like to see the Union Jack removed.

What do you think of the idea of replacing the Union Jack with both the Aboriginal and the Torres Strait Islander flags?

One country – three flags
p. 38

With the creation of ATSIC in 1990, the Torres Strait Islanders achieved official recognition and their flag has been given equal prominence with the Aboriginal flag. So it would be politically correct to replace the Union Jack with both flags, if this was to be considered at all.

Traumatic Experience versus Opportunity to Develop

Synopsis of the text

This short text refers to Harold Thomas, the designer of the Aboriginal flag. He thinks that the separation from his family gave him the opportunity to develop and thus to become the first Aboriginal to graduate from an Australian art school.

Assignments

Activities

1. How does Harold Thomas see his early separation from his parents?

The other side of the coin
p. 39

Harold Thomas sees both sides of the coin: on the one hand, the early separation from his parents was a traumatic experience for him. On the other hand, it gave him the opportunity to develop his abilities.

2. How did it influence his life?

His talent for painting was discovered at school. With the help of a scholarship he could go to art school and eventually get a university degree.

A case for gratitude? **p. 39**

Mr Thomas says that because he had been separated from his family he had the opportunity to develop and eventually to get a university degree. Should he be grateful for having had this chance?
The opposing issues are:
traumatic experience versus **opportunity to develop.**
Do the benefits outweigh the pains suffered? What do you think?

There is controversy about this question. Many white Australians believe that if the children had been left to live in the bush with their tribal families, they would still be there, illiterate and without any education. Many others are of the opinion that the state governments acted brutally, even criminally when they took the part-Aboriginal children away and that their behaviour is inexcusable.

Gratitude Wanted David McNicoll

Synopsis of the text

The columnist of *The Bulletin* is convinced that the Whites have done their best for the Blacks in recent times. The separation of part-Aboriginal babies from their families was done with the best motives. He thinks that Aboriginal people should show gratitude for what has been done for them.

Assignments

Activities

Thinking about interhuman relations **p. 40**

1. The columnist uses the word *best* twice: in the phrases "has done his best for the blacks" and "it was with the best motives". When people try to "do their best" for you, but the result is not what you want, how do you react to them?

David McNicoll is in line with the views expressed in the children's verse and by Governor Hindmarsh (see pp. 26-27). His ethnocentric attitude puts Aboriginal people in the wrong, as it is inconceivable to him that they do not appreciate the achievements of white civilization.

These phrases should sound quite familiar to the students. They will remember situations when others thought they knew what was *best* for them. They might have a lot to say about the possible outcome of such conflicting situations.

2. Is David McNicoll's disappointment at the Aboriginals' lack of gratitude justified?

If the columnist was broad-minded and could accept the fact that some Aboriginal people do not want to change their traditional way of life, there would be no reason for him to be disappointed or offended.

"They Have Every Reason to Be Grateful"

Synopsis of the text

The writer of this letter to the editor confirms Mr McNicoll's opinion that Aboriginal people have every reason to be grateful. In support of his statement he quotes the example of Lois O'Donoghue, a member of the *stolen generation,* who became foundation chairperson of ATSIC.

Assignments

Activities

Forming your own opinion p. 41

1. Have a close look at Mr Polya's assertion. Then comment on his opinion that it can be "justly stated" that Aboriginal people are so much better off today.

Mr Polya's letter to the editor contains unproven statements. To be "economically better off through welfare and other payments provided by courtesy of the Australian taxpayer" cannot be what Indigenous people strived for.

2. Just like Mr Harold Thomas, who says of himself that the separation from his family gave him the chance to go to university, Ms O'Donoghue had the chance to develop and to become a well-known political figure in Australia. Another case for gratitude? What is your opinion?

Obviously, Lois O'Donoghue could not have become foundation chairperson of ATSIC if she had not been brought up and educated in white institutions. On the other hand, the creation of agencies such as ATSIC resulted from the Aboriginals' wish for self-management, which is what they had when the First Fleet arrived. Therefore, Mr Polya should be more explicit about what the Aborigines are supposed to be grateful for.

The Fringe Dwellers Nene Gare

Author

The Fringe Dwellers (1961) was Nene Gare's (1919-1994) first published novel. It drew on her husband's experience as a district officer with the Native Welfare Department in WA from 1952-62. The novel was filmed in 1986.

Synopsis of the text

Trilby has just come back from her neighbour's with a pile of clothes. She is angry that Mrs Henwood dared give her her old clothes. Her sister thinks it was nice of her, while their mother has already put on a badly fitting cardigan she picked out of the pile.

Trilby becomes more and more furious until she takes the clothes, puts them into the dustbin, pours kerosene on them and burns them.

Assignments

While-reading tasks

p. 41 Why is Trilby so angry?

Trilby is angry because her neighbour did not stop throwing the clothes over her arm although she kept saying “no”.

p. 42 Does Noonah share Trilby’s opinion?

Noonah is of a different opinion. She thinks that some of the dresses will look nice on her sister if she takes them in at the waist.

p. 42 What do you think of Trilby’s opinion?

Trilby is convinced that her neighbour only gave her the clothes because she is Aboriginal and therefore expected to be grateful for anything given to her by white people. She is sure that Mrs Henwood would not have dreamed of giving her old clothes to a white neighbour.
The students will have to decide whether they agree with Trilby or whether she is being oversensitive because of her Aboriginality.

p. 42 What seems to be the mother’s standpoint in this conflict?

The mother has no problem wearing her neighbour’s old clothes. Besides, she is not yet aware of her daughter’s anger.

p. 43 What is Trilby going to do?

Trilby is obviously going to throw the clothes away or destroy them.

p. 43 What is Trilby’s reaction to the accident?

Trilby is in such a rage that she is unable to show any sympathy with her mother or to see to her burnt arm.

p. 43 What do we get to know about Mrs Henwood’s reaction?

Mrs Henwood does not understand what is going on in her neighbours’ garden. She seems to be shocked and embarrassed and disappears immediately.

Activities

Analysing the causes of conflicts p. 44

1. Study each of the characters carefully and find out what part they play in the conflict. Then decide who is responsible for this disastrous outcome and whether one single character can be blamed.

Trilby: proud, wants equal rights, radical, vengeful; her pride has been hurt by Mrs Henwood’s action of giving her her old clothes.

Noonah: moderate, understanding, cooperative; thinks that her sister is overreacting, tries to mediate.

Mrs Comeaway: simple-minded, no pride (in Trilby's eyes), pragmatic, naive; unknowingly provokes her daughter by wearing Mrs Henwood's old cardigan.

Mrs Henwood: wants to be friendly and helpful, shows goodwill by living in a *mixed area*, no open racist attitude, lacks empathy; arouses Trilby's anger by giving her her old clothes.

All the characters involved in the conflict act according to their personal views. Their individual motives are understandable. The conflict arises from the constellation of the characters. So it cannot be concluded that it is one single character's fault.

2. We must presume that Mrs Henwood acted with the best of intentions. What went wrong to make her benevolent gesture turn into a catastrophe, frustrating, hurting, or offending everybody who is involved?

Mrs Henwood seems to be absolutely pleased with herself (ll. 16-18). She is carried away and ignores Trilby's refusal. She only sees herself (ll. 53-55). She should have asked Trilby if she wanted the clothes and should have listened to her when she kept saying "no".

Getting to the core of the problem p. 44

1. It all seems to boil down to the question whether you have to be grateful for something that you were given but never asked for, something that was almost forced upon you because the giver thinks that it is good for you. If the answer to this question is *no*, is the giver's disappointment at your lack of gratitude justified?

This question sums up what has been found out before. The students should now discuss it on an abstract level.

2. What might have been different if Mrs Henwood had asked Trilby if she wanted the clothes and if she had accepted her *no* without being offended?

If Mrs Henwood had asked Trilby if she wanted the clothes, Trilby would have felt that Mrs Henwood was taking her seriously. She would have felt respected by her. Mrs Henwood, on the other hand, would have spared herself her disappointment and the shock she must have had at seeing Trilby's reaction.

3. What might be different if the white Australians asked the black Australians what they want instead of assuming that what is good for themselves and makes them happy must be good for the Blacks, too?

If the non-Indigenous Australians accepted the fact that the Indigenous Australians want to be happy in their own way, according to their customs and traditions, they would spare themselves many frustrations. Some Aboriginal people want to live like white people, but some do not. The white Australians should not feel rejected or offended by the latter ones, but accept them on equal terms.

Chapter 5: Walking Together –

The Reconciliation Process

Vorbemerkungen zum Kapitel

Kapitel 5 setzt sich mit dem langwierigen „Reconciliation Process“ auseinander. Es enthält einige sprachlich schwierige, für die Schülerinnen und Schüler möglicherweise weniger interessante Texte, die aber für das Verständnis der gegenwärtigen Situation in Australien von großer Bedeutung sind.
Es handelt sich um die Gerichtsurteile im *Mabo* und *Wik Case.* Bei der Darstellung dieser Sachverhalte kann auf die Verwendung von Fachbegriffen wie *native title, common law, pastoral lease* etc., deren Bedeutung in Infoboxen erklärt wird, nicht verzichtet werden.
Bei der Vermittlung dieses Stoffes könnte sich der/die Unterrichtende des Lehrervortrages bedienen, indem er/sie die wichtigen Fakten zusammenfasst und dem Kurs vorträgt. Die Schülerinnen und Schüler könnten diesen Teil des Kapitels im Folgenden zu Referenzzwecken benutzen, wenn ihnen die Bedeutung eines Begriffes/Sachverhaltes nicht mehr gegenwärtig ist.
Die beiden Cartoons zum Thema *Reconciliation* sind für die Schülerinnen und Schüler sicher leichter zugänglich. Sie veranschaulichen, wie ablehnend bzw. misstrauisch sich die beiden Seiten gegenüberstehen.
Die beiden Texte über Grabschändungen in Tasmanien und die sehr zögerliche Herausgabe der in Museen gelagerten sterblichen Überreste im vergangenen Jahrhundert verstorbener Aborigines beleuchten das Thema aus einer anderen Richtung. Ebenso wie bei den Cartoons sollten die Schülerinnen und Schüler auch hier erkennen, wie schwierig sich der Aussöhnungsprozess gestaltet.
Um das Kapitel abzuschließen, sollte man die Bilder auf Seite 57 für sich sprechen lassen. Der E-Gitarre-Spieler im „Steinzeitdress“ fordert Spontanäußerungen geradezu heraus.

Start here

A united Australia? ➤ **p. 45**

Do you believe that the reconciliation process will bring black and white Australians closer together?

After what the students have learned so far about the difficult relationship between black and white Australians, they might be rather pessimistic about the reconciliation process. They should have some ideas, though, about what can be done to relieve the existing tension.

Pat Dodson – A Creative Mind

Synopsis of the text

This article from *The Bulletin* informs the readers about Pat Dodson, the first chairperson of the Council for Aboriginal Reconciliation. In December 1996 he was nominated one of Australia's most creative minds by the magazine.

Assignments

While-reading tasks

p. 47

Explain the examples given by Mr Dodson.

The first example is about a white Australian soldier who, of his own accord, made a plaque bearing the names of Aboriginal soldiers who went to war. He negotiated with the local authorities to have it erected in a central place.
The second example deals with the serious problem of Aboriginal deaths in custody (see infobox p. 47) and the ill-treatment Aboriginal people receive while they are in custody. It conforms to Pat Dodson's idea of reconciliation for the parties involved in this conflict to start talking about ways of improving the situation.

p. 47

What is *reconciliation* for him?

It is a simple idea which must be translated into action at grass-roots level.

Activities

A point for discussion p. 47

Why do you think Pat Dodson was nominated one of Australia's ten most creative minds?

The magazine obviously wanted to draw attention to the reconciliation process and emphasize its importance by nominating the chairperson of the Council for Aboriginal Reconciliation. (In 1993, the *Australian* newspaper named Eddie Mabo their *Australian of the Year*, see infobox p. 48.)

Creative exercise: preparing a speech p. 47

Imagine you are a white Australian wanting to give a speech in support of the Council for Aboriginal Reconciliation. What would you say? What could be your interest in the reconciliation process?

If the students are familiar with the techniques of political speeches, they might like to perform this speech on an affective level. The speaker might appeal to the emotions of the audience, which should be imagined to be predominantly white.

Here are some possible issues:

- we cannot have the world point their fingers at us because of the way we treat our Indigenous people;

- we have no right to denounce human rights abuses in other countries if we commit them in our own country;
- Australia never has been and never will be a racist country. We are a multi-cultural society and we feel that our cultural diversity enriches our daily lives;
- we therefore have an interest in preserving what is left of Aboriginal culture and traditions;
- Australia has become very popular with tourists from all over the world. Do we want our visitors to go back home with the impression that we allow our Indigenous people to live in squalor and neglect? Do we want them to believe that the tolerance we display is really nothing but indifference?
- in all the wars against tyranny and despotism this century has seen, Australia has always been on the side of democracy and has always fought for the right cause. Should we not act according to the same principle in our own country?
- after all, our country represents one of the world's oldest democracies. We want social justice in this beautiful country of ours, and this is why the reconciliation process must go on.

Mabo and the Fight for Native Title

Synopsis of the text

The *Mabo Case* goes back to Eddie Mabo, one of five Torres Strait Islanders who went to court with the aim of having their rights over their land recognized. The High Court decision is of great importance. It does away with the former assumption of *Terra Nullius* and gives Aboriginal people the right to claim *native title* to their land.

Assignments

While-reading tasks

p. 48

Why did the five Torres Strait Islanders go to court?

They went to court in order to claim native title (see p. 49) to their land.

p. 48

Explain the most important outcome of the High Court decision.

The High Court ruled that the doctrine of *Terra Nullius* was wrong and recognized the Indigenous people's rights to claim native title to their land.

p. 48

What rights does the *Native Title Act 1993* give to Indigenous people?
What rights does it not give to them?

The act gives Indigenous people the right to claim native title to land they have always been connected with, in accordance with their traditions. However, it does not give them the right to claim privately owned land.

Activity

In 1992, for the first time since the arrival of the First Fleet, it was recognized that the concept of *terra nullius* was wrong and that Aboriginal people had rights over their land. Black Australia, above all the Land Councils, celebrated this victory. But what do you suppose white Australia said to the High Court decision?

Becoming aware of the importance of the Mabo decision p. 49

There was consent and disapproval, depending on people's political views. The historian and parlamentarian Geoffrey Blainey, for example, believes that the Native Title Act is an "ingenious form of racial discrimination" (meaning: discrimination against white Australians): "The Native Title Act rests on a genuine concern for principle and yet judged by that principle it might well be called unprincipled. It embodies a crusade against racial discrimination and yet it sets up a new form of racial discrimination. Land blessed by the Native Title Act is specifically placed under the control of people of one race. It is land with racial cords attached. [...] As the Native Title Act runs its course, vast areas of Australia will be reserved permanently for people of one race. Would the authors of this revolutionary Act think it also appropriate if land around Circular Quay [Sydney] was reserved in perpetuity for people of, say, Irish birth, or if land in Canberra is to be owned henceforth only by people of white ancestry?"

("Black future" by Geoffrey Blainey, in: *The Bulletin with Newsweek*, April 8, 1997, p. 23)

Reconciliation – No!

Assignments

Activity

What reasons might white Australians have for not wanting to proceed with reconciliation?

Understanding other people's motives p. 49

Pauline Hanson, founder and leader of the *One Nation* Party (right wing): "I have said that the concept of reconciliation is tarnished and should be abandoned, and I do not retreat from this position. Reconciliation was designed to make today's white Australians plead guilty for what happened in the distant past and to pay compensation. [...] A process of reconciliation forced down mainstream Australia's throat will be bitterly resented and will ensure that divisions already evident in our society remain."

("Reconciliation is a dirty word" by Pauline Hanson, in: *The Bulletin with Newsweek*, June 11, 1996, p. 60)

The *Wik Case*

Synopsis of the text

The *Wik Case* deals with land that has been leased to pastoralists. The High Court decided that native title rights continue at the same time the land is leased to someone else.

Assignments

While-reading tasks

p. 50

Why is the *Wik Case* so important?

The *Wik Case* is so important because the High Court ruled that Native Title rights could continue at the same time that the land was leased to somebody else (see infobox: Pastoral leases cover about 40 per cent of the continent).

p. 50

In your opinion, what should the government do?

White Australians might need more information about what Native Title means and how it affects them. The High Court decisions might not have been sufficiently explained to the people. Some, like Geoffrey Blainey (see p. 57), for example, think that they were based on the wrong facts: "At least two judges of the High Court appear not to have completed their research on the facts of the Aboriginals' dispossession, facts which they said were 'of critical importance' in their deciding whether native title still cxists. [They] did not know that disease was the main killer of Aborigines. They preferred to pin the blame on the British and to look for ways of compensating Aborigines for what they called 'a national legacy of unutterable shame'."

("Black future" by Geoffrey Blainey, in: *The Bulletin with Newsweek*, April 8, 1997, p. 22)

A Look Inside the Prime Minister's Mind ...

Assignments

Activities

Forming one's opinion about the difficult process of reconciliation **p. 51**

1. Collect all the information contained in the cartoon.

The picture shows the Australian prime minister:

- the chair is too big for him
- the desk is too high for him
- there is nothing but the concept of *Terra Nullius* in his head
- he looks completely helpless.

2. What point does the cartoonist, Kevin Lindeberg, want to make?

The prime minister is not ready for reconciliation as he still clings to the out-dated doctrine of *Terra Nullius*. Besides, the task is too difficult for him and he is not competent enough to do it.

3. Whose opinion is he likely to represent?

The cartoonist obviously represents the Aborigines' point of view. It was under Prime Minister Paul Keating (Labor Party) that the legislative framework for the *Native Title Act 1993* was constructed. When the conservative John Howard (Liberal Party) won the elections in 1996, the Indigenous Australians feared that the reconciliation process might slow down.

4. This cartoon appeared in an Aboriginal newspaper in October 1997 when the decade-long reconciliation process was more than half way through. How do you estimate the chances of a successful reconciliation? Will the centenary of the Australian Federation on January 1, 2001, be celebrated by a united Australia?

Whatever one might think about the chances of a successful reconciliation, it should be clear that the reconciliation process cannot be completed within a decade. The main thing is that it has been started and that more and more attention will be drawn to it as we approach the year 2001.

Grave-Robbing in Tasmania

Brendon Bowes

Synopsis of the text

There was a great interest in Aboriginal remains. Influenced by the ideas of Darwinism, some scientists believed the Tasmanian Aborigines to be the missing link between apes and men. Therefore their remains were exhumed and exhibited in museums in Tasmania and abroad.
Truganini, believed to be the last Tasmanian fullblood Aboriginal, hoped to escape this fate. However, after a Christian burial, her body was exhumed with the approval of the Tasmanian government, and her skeleton displayed in the Hobart museum.

Assignments

While-reading tasks

What was Truganini afraid of?

p. 52

Truganini was afraid of being exhumed after her burial. She was terrified by the idea that the scientists might cut her body up and display her skeleton in a museum.

p. 52 ➤ Who was William Lanne?

William Lanne was Truganini's companion. He was believed to be the last full-blood male Tasmanian Aboriginal.

p. 52 ➤ What does "specimens" mean in this context?

In the same way that science museums display the skeletons of extinct species, they were keen on displaying the skeletal remains of Aboriginal people who, they expected, would soon die out.

p. 52 ➤ What did Crowther and his son do?

Crowther and his son went to the morgue where Lanne's body was lying. They wanted to take his skull. So they cut the body open, took the skull and replaced it with the skull of another corpse in order to hide what they had done.

p. 53 ➤ Was Stokell's suspicion justified?

Stokell's suspicion was justified. Crowther had invited him to dine at his house so that Stokell would not be able to get at the body in the morgue before him.

p. 53 ➤ How do you explain Stokell's behaviour?

The race with Crowther, who at first beat him to the body, must have driven Stokell into a frenzy.

p. 53 ➤ What did Crowther's grandson do in 1908?

Together with a fellow medical student, Crowther's grandson robbed Aboriginal graves and exhumed twelve bodies. The skeletal remains were then sent to museums.

p. 54 ➤ What do you think of this justification?

It sounds a rather week excuse. The enlargement of science should not be placed above human dignity and the respect of the dead.

Activities

Drawing conclusions p. 54 ➤ Seeing how the people who pretended to be working for "the enlargement of science" pounced on the corpses to tear them apart, what must have been their interest in Aboriginal people? What does their behaviour tell us about them?

The scientists were influenced by the ideas of Darwinism which made them believe that the Tasmanian race was the missing link between apes and men (see ll. 33-34). Therefore they did not really see the Tasmanian Aborigines as human beings.

Project: Darwinism p. 54 ➤ Find out what *Darwinism* is about and how its ideas influenced the white Australians in their treatment of the Aboriginals.

Basically, Darwinism is the theory of the origin of animal and plant species by evolution through the process of natural selection. The students might go on from here and show the interrelation between this theory and the treatment of the Tasmanian Aborigines by the Whites.

Death Bill Neidjie

Synopsis of the text

Bill Neidjie emphasizes the importance of being buried in the proper place. When he is buried he will go back to his family and become earth again.

Aboriginal Remains Back Where They Belong

Synopsis of the text

After long and painful negotiations with the University of Edinburgh, a delegation of Indigenous Australians finally succeeded in bringing the remains of 297 Aboriginal people back to Australia so that they could be buried in their proper places.

Assignments

While-reading tasks

What is the solemn occasion described in this article?

p. 55

It is the return of the skeletal remains of almost 300 Aborigines that had been sent to the University of Edinburgh.

Why are they only "almost" home?

p. 56

The skeletal remains have to be identified and returned to their community of origin so that they can be buried in their proper place.

Why is it so important to return the skeletal remains to their proper place?

p. 56

The skeletal remains have to be buried in the proper place so that they can be reunited with the land from which these people originated and that they can return to the spirit world.

Activity

The campaign for the return of other remains still continues today. What might account for the reluctance of the museums to give the skeletal remains of Aboriginal people back to their families so that they can be buried in their proper place?

The difficult process of reconciliation p. 56

The museums maintain that it is important to keep the skeletal remains for scientific research. The question arises whether the scientists' attitude has changed in the last ninety years since Crowther's grandson robbed Aboriginal graves for the "enlargement of science".

Living Black in a White Society

Synopsis of the text

This short text shows how Aboriginal people try to cope with *Australia Day,* the anniversary of the arrival of the First Fleet in 1788. They call it *Survival Day* and stage big concerts to celebrate the survival of Aboriginal culture.

Additional Texts

Aboriginal Humour

ute (Aus. inf.) utility, a small truck

One time we were going from Quorn back to Leigh Creek with my old Uncle Dan and we were in this old *Chrysler* ute. Me and my mate, old Alec Patterson, we were standing up in the back and the car didn't have any brakes on it. He was going out of the town real steady at first and as soon as he got out of town past the railway line, he let her go then. When he let her go this bloke came along with a motor bike and horses and he couldn't pull up. That was funny, that.

I'll tell you a good one, Russell Fazulla was coming from Quorn to Port Augusta and he bumped into my brother-in-law, Phil Jackson. He was out of petrol. Russell said, 'What's wrong with you Phil?' He said, 'I've run out of petrol.' Russell said, 'Have you got a hose and that,' so he siphoned some out into one of those old time flagon bottles. Russell said, 'I can give you a flagon, that'll get you into Stirling.' He poured that petrol but kept half of it and screwed the top back on. Russel said, 'Why don't you put the lot in?' He said, 'No, I'll save some just in case I run out again.' That's real Irish isn't it?

station a privately owned rural establishment for raising sheep or cattle
jocks tight-fitting underpants for men

One time it was real hot weather out on the station and I used to sleep with just my jocks on and my mate used to sleep fully clothed. I said, 'Ain't you hot? Why don't you put your shorts on or something?'. He said, 'No, if I die tonight, I want them to see me fully clothed.'

Murray Wilton

Easter Story

When I was little, in Grade one or two, we used to have a little garden each. I had a strawberry patch, I don't know why? Probably because they looked pretty I suppose. Anyway, one old lady, the teacher, called Mrs Sweet, she said, 'All you kids. You have to go out and make a nest and put your names there so that Easter bunny will know what to give you.' Being kids, we didn't understand that people put the eggs in there. Anyway, I was thinking 'Easter bunny with eggs?' 'You'll get chocolate eggs' she told the class.
At dinner time I rode home on my little bike and got half a dozen rabbit traps, brought them back and set them around the strawberry patch

because I was going to catch the Easter bunny and take the eggs. Real devious! That afternoon the poor old lady came in and she had the heels broken off her shoes and dust all up her dress and she pointed at me. I thought, 'What are you thinking of me for?' and she said, 'Come out here' and I got the biggest caning because she got caught in the traps I set. I realized then that the teacher put the eggs in there so I learnt a lesson from that. It was dumb wasn't it?

Buck McKenzie

devious *verschlagen, hinterhältig.*

Chapter 6: "Put Two and Two Together" – Becoming "Two-Ways Strong"

Vorbemerkungen zum Kapitel

Das letzte Kapitel zeigt an einigen Beispielen, wie indigene Australier heute in der weißen Gesellschaft leben, wie sie ihre Identität wahren und wie sie ihre Zukunft sehen. Den Schülerinnen und Schülern sollte vermittelt werden, dass es sich dabei immer nur um Einzelbeispiele handeln kann. Denn wie der vorliegende Reader zeigt, gibt es sehr viele individuelle Ausprägungen persönlicher Lebenswege, die sich nicht über einen Kamm scheren lassen. So gibt es neben den im letzten Kapitel vorgestellten „Karrieren" auch heute noch Aborigines, die ihr traditionelles Leben weiterführen oder bewusst dazu zurückgekehrt sind.

Start here

Thinking about the future p. 58

Mr McKenzie stresses the importance of education for Aboriginal children. According to him, they must learn the black man's as well as the white man's way. Do you agree with him? How do you see the future of the Aboriginal peoples and Torres Strait Islanders in Australia?

Buck McKenzie advocates biculturalism for Aboriginal children. The course should discuss his opinion. Students originating from other countries, who practise a similar kind of biculturalism in Germany, might contribute to the discussion by telling the course about their personal experiences with being bicultural.

The Double Life of Bruce Martin – Thorough Biculturalism

Kerry-Anne Walsh

Synopsis of the text

This text from *The Bulletin* is an example of how an Aboriginal teenager manages to live in two worlds. He lives with his white father and step-mother in Canberra where he attends a public school. But he spends his holidays with his mother's clan in North Queensland and takes part in the traditional life of his mother's extended family.

Assignments

While-reading tasks

p. 59

Explain this utopia.

Bruce Martin manages to live comfortably in two worlds: that of his tribal family in Cape York and that of white society in Canberra.

p. 60

How has Bruce fused both his worlds?

When Bruce is up north, he is part of his Aboriginal family. When he is down south, he is part of the white system. He seems to have no problems with his two selves.

p. 60

What type of student is he?

On top of being bilingual and bicultural and doing well at school, he is an accomplished sportsman.

p. 60

How do his classmates see him?

His classmates see him as a friend, not as an Aboriginal.

p. 61

Would you act like Bruce's father?

Bruce's father obviously sees an advantage in offering his son access to two different cultures. He thinks that this will enrich his personal life. The students might not be of the same opinion. Some might hold the view that it rather confuses or weakens a child to be brought up with differing cultural values.

Activities

Arranging your items
p. 61

Check your list and arrange your items in two columns, each referring to one of the two different worlds of Bruce Martin. You might need a third column representing the synthesis of both worlds.

Up North

- lives in the world of his traditional people
- lives part of the year with his mother's Wolomby clan on the Cape York peninsula in Far North Queensland
- lives a traditional life of hunting and fishing within the complex extended family units
- at home in the spiritual and ceremonial world of his people
- part of the family

Synthesis

- able to live comfortably in two worlds
- has fused both his worlds: has two selves, one for the north, and one for the south, which don't compete or clash
- it's part of his life
- straddles both worlds so easily
- thoroughly bicultural

Down South

- the best that white society has to offer
- spends the rest of the time with his white father David in suburban Canberra
- accomplished sportsman and scholar
- dons the uniform of one of Canberra's top private schools
- learns how to compete in the world of white people
- speaks with a cultured accent
- is part of the white system
- first Aboriginal student to attend Canberra Boys' Grammar School
- has represented the ACT in swimming, plays basketball for his school and this year won the school's cross country race
- is just one of the boys in year 7
- catches up on work when he returns, and must fulfil all his academic requirements

Summing up the contents p. 61

According to the writer of this article, why does Bruce have the best of both worlds, and how does his biculturalism enrich his personal life?

Bruce goes to one of the top private schools in Canberra where he gets the best education that white society has to offer. When he stays with his Aboriginal family in North Queensland, he learns different skills and gets a different insight into life. So he is more experienced and better educated than other boys his age.

The world upside down? p. 61

There has been a lot of moving in Bruce's life. In Australia, moving seems to be linked to embarking on a new life. But there is more to it.

1. Look at your list again and say which part of Bruce's life belongs to *Up North* and which part belongs to *Down South*.

Up North Bruce leads a traditional life with his extended family. It is a life of hunting, fishing and spiritual ceremonies.

Down South he goes to school to get a good education; he has to study hard and learns how to compete in the world of white people.

Up North seems to be all fun, while *Down South* seems to be all work.

2. What do *north* and *south* stand for in Australia as compared to Europe?

In *Down Under* the world is upside down when seen with European eyes.
While most of the big cities and industries are in the "cold" south, the north stands for nice weather, beautiful landscapes and a casual lifestyle. It is the place where the southerners like to spend their holidays.

Your opinion p. 61

The second paragraph stresses one of the main differences between these two worlds:
sharing with his extended family versus **competing with his white classmates.**
Do you think it weakens a person to learn such contradictory strategies or does it rather strengthen them?

According to the following article, it strengthens a person when they are brought up with two different cultures.

"Two-Ways Strong"

Synopsis of the text

The author of this article fights against the myth that Aboriginal people lose their culture if they go through the European tertiary education system. He/She is of the opinion that the fact that there is a growing number of Aboriginal professionals proves the opposite. The writer claims that having learned two systems and having had both an Aboriginal and a European education, they are better educated than non-Aboriginal people and have become "two-ways strong".

Assignments

Activity

Becoming aware of the strength of biculturalism p. 62

Maybe you know people to whom this definition also applies. Or maybe you are yourself “two-ways strong”, strong in two cultures. Has it ever occurred to you that such people are better educated than their colleagues who are strong in only one culture, as the author of this article claims?

Students originating from countries with different political systems or who have been brought up with non-Christian religious beliefs might feel that this definition applies to them. They will be used to the fact that their biculturalism has not been considered an advantage in Germany. They should therefore readily identify with the opinion expressed in this article. But it might also help the German students realize that learning about different cultures makes them become “more-ways strong”.

The Exhausted Optimist Peter Wear

Synopsis of the text

The Aboriginal lawyer and land rights activist Noel Pearson also has become “two-ways strong”. He used his knowledge to help his people fight for their rights. But now he wants to leave his home country in North Queensland and work as a lawyer in a white firm in Melbourne.

Assignments

While-reading tasks

Who is Noel Pearson? p. 62

Noel Pearson is a well-known Aboriginal lawyer who worked for the Land Council (see p. 47) in Cairns and negotiated the Native Title Act with the government.

What might he mean by this description? p. 63

Noel Pearson has fought for the land rights movement with all his might and is now exhausted but still optimistic that the Native Title Act will show results.

How did Pearson react to the shock of entering white society? p. 63

When Pearson learned that the Aborigines were the most hated group in Australian society, he became very ambitious and wanted to show his white classmates that he could do better than they did.

p. 63
How does he judge the reconciliation process?

Pearson thinks that laws alone will change nothing if the white people are not willing to reconcile and compromise. So far he does not see enough willingness.

p. 63
How has Pearson become "two-ways strong"?

His father taught him how to catch fish with a spear (see picture of Bruce Martin on page 59, student's book) and never to miss his target, not even in muddy water. He has shown the same determination in his profession as a lawyer and in his political work.

Activity

A matter of conscience p. 64

According to the article, Noel Pearson has worked for the Land Rights Movement "for all of his adult life". His departure caused shock and dismay. Is he entitled to move down to Melbourne to start a brilliant career in commercial law, or does he have a moral obligation towards his fellow Aboriginals who desperately need him in the Land Rights Movement? Has Pearson become "over-strong" in white culture and is now behaving "white"?

The students should discuss the question whether the individual's right of self-realization carries more weight than their moral obligations toward society.

A Letter from England

Synopsis of the text

The letter writer refers to the event on January 26, 1988, when Burnum Burnum planted the Aboriginal flag on the white cliffs of Dover and claimed Britain in the name of the Australian Aboriginal people. The letter writer is getting impatient because the invasion still has not taken place. He thinks that the Aboriginal way of life might help his "tarnished country" to survive.

Assignments

While-reading tasks

p. 64
Who might the letter writer be?

The letter writer reveals himself to be an Englishman who reminds Burnum Burnum of his "invasion" in 1988.

p. 64
Why does he write to Burnum Burnum?

He informs Burnum Burnum that he accepts his claim and is ready to submit to him.

What is the writer's attitude towards Aboriginal people?

p. 65

The writer thinks that he and his fellow countrymen should learn from Aboriginal people how to look after the land.

Has the writer's aim become clear?

p. 65

Adam Stout obviously is a telling name. The writer uses this pseudonym and expresses his loyalty to emphasize the fact that he welcomes the Indigenous people of Australia to control his country.

Activities

1. In what way does the form of this letter correspond to the *happening* staged by Burnum Burnum?

Ways of expressing one's opinion p. 65

In response to the *one-man show* staged by Burnum Burnum, the letter writer takes it upon himself to act on behalf of his country.

2. How do you evaluate this way of dealing with the problem?

This letter deals with the British invasion and Burnum Burnum's reaction to it in a witty, light-hearted way. It might relieve the students or amuse them after all the (unsolvable) problems that had to be dealt with throughout this course.

Conclusion Bill Neidjie

Synopsis of the text

Bill Neidjie concludes that all people, no matter what their skin colour might be or what language they might speak, have the same feelings and are the same.

Additional Text

The following text is the epilogue of Sally Morgan's book *Wanamurraganya, The Story of Jack McPhee.* Sally Morgan met Jack McPhee, her grandfather through Aboriginal kinship, when she travelled to the north of Western Australia in search of her extended family, while researching her first book, *My Place.*

Epilogue Sally Morgan

I've had a think, and before I [Jack McPhee] say anything, I want to say this. The way I see things is based on the way I've had to live, please remember that.

station a privately owned rural establishment for raising sheep or cattle
damper a bush bread made from a simple flour and water dough, cooked in the coals or in a camp oven
roo kangaroo
squatter (formerly) one who settled on Crown land to run stock, esp. sheep, initially without government permission, but later with a lease or license
fella man, bloke

I want to talk about stations. They were built on black labour. On sour bread, damper, roo meat and whippings. The squatter had it hard too, because life in those days was hard, but they made money out of it. Two generations on, their families are all right, ours aren't. Many of them are now wealthy men with land and businesses and respect, we have nothing.

I can only explain it like this. Two friends of mine were working on a station. The manager, who was an okay fella, went away and put a new bloke in charge. There was a good garden there, my friend looked after it while his wife worked in the house. Now the new boss loved watermelon and my friend had some in the garden. He was told he wasn't allowed to have any of those melons, even though my friend had grown them himself. Instead, when the boss had eaten the good part, he would throw him the leftovers. For years the whiteman's been getting the sweet part of the melon and the blackman, if he's lucky, has had to be content with leftovers.

I can honestly say that I have tried very hard in my life to live quietly and to better myself and my family. When I was just a native I was told that if I wanted to get on in the world I had to become a whiteman, but when I tried to do that people would look at me and say, 'Oh you're just a native!'

language here: Aboriginal language

Some people think all Aborigines are the same, yet we have different tribal groups, different languages, different customs. Our colour isn't even the same, some of us are black, some are brown, some are only light. Some of us can speak language and some know only English; some can read and write and some can't. Some of us are no-hopers and alcoholics, and others are working men who know right from wrong. People see a few rotten apples and write us off. I've known whitemen who were bastards and I've known whitemen who were the best mates a man could have. I'm sick of people thinking we all look and think the same. A man should be judged on his own and not as part of a group.

mate friend, pal (used by male speakers referring to men)
Mulba the name by which Aboriginal people of the Port Hedland / Marble Bar area of Western Australia refer to themselves

Now, about Mulba things. I think it's very sad that some of our people feel ashamed of the old culture, especially our languages and dancing. I can speak five Aboriginal languages and I can sing in seven. I know many Mulbas who can speak their language but won't. Sometimes when I'm sitting in the South Hedland shopping centre, I wait until I see some of my countrymen coming and then I call out to them in language. They get very embarrassed. I tell them I'm not ashamed of my language and they shouldn't be either. I'll speak my language anywhere.

to run sb. down *jemanden schlechtmachen*

You see, their idea is this. They think if they talk language the white people might think they're running them down. Over the years I've seen the same thing happen at corroboree time. White people are very interested in corroborees, but my people get worried about singing in language in case someone says, 'Oh speak bloody English will ya?!'

For many years there was ill feeling in the North between black and white. No one wanted us to go up in the world, we were classed next to a dog. I'm happy to say that's changing. However, I don't agree with some of the black people who won't speak to white people. They're getting silly themselves now. They blame the white people for everything, especially the past, but I think there are some things happening now that they're responsible for. Young people drinking and stealing, old people gambling everything, mothers and fathers not wanting to work or look after their kids. We had none of that in my day.

It's hard because Mulbas see things differently. We'd rather lend twenty dollars to someone than pay the rent. If people owe us money and won't pay we just walk away. We've got to be in a group all the time, we won't spread out and make an independent living for ourselves. The grandmothers won't say no to anything. They keep taking in all the children the young people don't want instead of making them care for those kids themselves.

Also, if things are all right now like people say, then why are all these boys dying in gaol? I just can't understand that and it really worries me. I am very worried about the young Aboriginal boys and girls and what's going to become of them if they keep on the way they are. I know there are some good ones who try their best, that's why I'm going to make a scholarship, to help the ones that are trying to help themselves. I want to do that, and I want to be remembered as someone who made mistakes like everyone else, but who came through in the end and did something good for his people.

I'm roughly eighty-four now and I've been through a lot in my life. I have to tell you that it's only as you get to the end of your life that you start to realise what things are really important to you. I've been through the Exemption Certificate and Citizenship and I've struggled to live up to the whiteman's standard, but here I am, old, and good for nothing, and what keeps coming back to me? Dances, singing, stories the old people used to tell. Every night I lie in bed and sing myself to sleep with all my old corroboree songs. I go over and over them and I remember that part of my life. They're the things I love, they're the things I miss.

Exemption Certificate and Citizenship
also: Citizenship Certificate – a certificate issued to Aborigines deemed to have been "civilized", i.e. those who had adopted a "European life-style". It entitled them to vote, drink alcohol, use hotels and otherwise exercise the rights enjoyed by other Australians.

Teil III

Klausurbeispiele

Klausur 1

Racism That Stalks WA

Glen Healey Hood

Today's columnist, Glen Healey Hood, is a psychologist who has worked for UNICEF. She moved to Switzerland in 1958 and returned to Perth in 1988, bringing together more than 30 organisations to form the WA Coalition for Humane Juvenile Justice.

I want to tell a story. A true one:

Many years ago, the white invaders who came to this land with their "gift of civilisation" began committing atrocities on the healthy, harmonious people who had inhabited this land for 40,000 years.

We whites have now been here just 200 years and atrocities in one form or another continue. Although we have not sought the agreement of the people to whom this land legally belongs, we want to deprive them of their sacred places and make massive fortunes out of them.

Do they desecrate our churches and cemeteries?

I cannot go into detail of the savage atrocities committed during the invasion by the white settlers because they would be unprintable for a newspaper and it would pain me too greatly.

Certainly, they were far, far worse than atrocities committed in Serbian or nazi concentration camps. They were demonic, sexually depraved and the details are well documented. Governor Stirling was among those who authorised a massacre, the battle of Pinjarra in 1834.

We have even neglected to give these people a name. "Aborigine" means the indigenous person of any country.

There were originally a million of them, but the delicate ecological balance that once sustained their lifestyle in paradise was destroyed by the British in six months. Resistance to white disease was low and the remnants of the Aboriginal population were shunted into reserves and camps where they lived in squalor on "white" rations of white flour, white sugar and tea.

Many were taken prisoner and chained together. The surviving children were herded into "white" schools and indoctrinated. Unofficial "nigger hunts" were conducted by groups of racist whites until the 1930s, and there were Aborigines unfortunate enough to "be in the way" of British nuclear bomb blasts in South Australia in the 1950s.

In WA, the Aborigines who had influence among their people were marched great distances in their chains to be hanged where St George's Cathedral now stands. Or they were shipped to Rottnest to undergo brutalisation and death there.

Still today, Aborigines undergo brutalisation at the hands of the police, when they are beaten by several bullies at a time in police cells, or they are insulted, yelled at and hit by police who enter their homes.

Youths do not dare to venture out of their own four walls for fear of being picked up and brutalised. They are called "black dogs", "niggers" and are even assaulted if they wear a pair of sunglasses.

One of the greatest tragedies of the Aboriginal people is the lost generation: the youth who seek to find their parents, their brothers and sisters, from whom they were wrenched as babies to be indoctrinated with "white civilisation".

Still today, a neo-fascist style mob can assemble in the grounds of Parliament House in Perth with nooses, just like at Ku Klux Klan lynchings, and cry for the floggings and hangings of yesteryear. To gain their votes, an inhuman law was passed to take us legally back to yesteryear.

Still today, white people from the most affluent suburbs of Perth, people who have never known what it is like to be hungry, homeless, stateless and despised, still today they write to newspapers demanding beatings of the children of this white, racist occupied land.

Why then do we express outrage at what has been done in Chile, East Timor, Bosnia and Ukraine when we do not even acknowledge what we have committed here: the worst human rights abuses this world has ever known.

Annotations

to stalk to spread over (a place, here: Western Australia) in a menacing or grim manner – 12 **to deprive** to stop from having, to dispossess – 25 **depraved** morally bad, perverted – 34 **to sustain** to keep in existence – 37 **remnant** small remaining number – 38 **to shunt** (inf.) *abschieben* – 39 **in squalor** in an unpleasant state because of neglect and poverty – 55 **Rottnest** island near Perth – 59 **bully** a person who hurts weaker people – 69 **lost generation** here: stolen generation – 76 **noose** a loop in the end of a rope, used for hangings – 78 **yesteryear** (fml.) the past

Assignments

1. What "story" does the columnist tell her readers? (Inhalt)
2. This column may be divided into two parts. Say where the second part starts and sum up the main information given in each part. (Inhalt)
3. How does the fact that this is a column, and not a news story for example, influence the way in which the writer presents her ideas to the readers? (Form)
4. What stylistic and rhetorical devices does the columnist employ to appeal to her readers? (Form)
5. The introductory note to this column informs the readers that Mrs Hood is the founder of an organization called "West Australian Coalition for Humane Juvenile Justice". According to this article, what do you suppose are the aims of this organization? (Stellungnahme)
6. What is your opinion of Mrs Hood's view that "the worst human rights abuses this world has ever known" (lines 93-94) have taken place in Australia? (Stellungnahme)

Solutions

Die folgenden Lösungsvorschläge stellen lediglich eine Auswahl möglicher Antworten dar. Da nur die einzelnen Kurslehrerinnen und -lehrer wissen, auf welche Voraussetzungen und Vorkenntnisse sie zurückgreifen können (z.B. bei Formfragen), kann es sich bei den Lösungsvorschlägen nur um Beispiele handeln.

1. The students sum up the information given in the "story".
2. Part one: line 1 to line 56, part two: line 57 to the end. The students sum up the main aspects of each part of the text.

3. The column, in contrast to the news story, deals with the topic on an intellectual as well as on an affective level. The columnist has the possibility
   – to mislead the readers as to her true intention
   – to express her personal opinion and be partial
   – to accuse (without giving proof)
   – to give her judgement on the events referred to
   – to use persuasive and provocative language
   – to use emotional language in order to show her own feelings and to appeal to the readers' emotions, etc.

4. The columnist wants to arouse the readers' interest by telling a "true story". She prepares the readers for the fact that this is their own story (**I** want → the white invaders → **we** whites). She uses
   – irony (ll. 3-4, l. 48, ll. 53-54)
   – rhetorical questions (ll. 15-16, ll. 89-94)
   – repetition of words (e.g. "atrocities": ll. 4, 8, 17-18, 23)
   – parallel sentence structure/anaphora (l. 57, l. 74, l. 82, ll. 85-86)
   – comparison to other historical events (ll. 23-24, ll. 90-91)
   – symbolic language (e.g. "white")
   – passive voice to stress the victimization of Aboriginal people, etc.

5. The aims of this organization seem to be the following:
   – to fight against police despotism with regard to young Aborigines
   – to ban corporal punishment and abusive language used by the police
   – safety in the streets
   – an unprejudiced, non-racist environment
   – laws to protect Aboriginal people
   – an unbiased parliament
   – social equality, etc.

6. The reference to the nazi concentration camps and wars taking place in Europe brings the topic closer to the focus of interest of students in Germany. They should express their opinions about the columnist's idea by producing an argumentative text.

Klausur 2

An Aboriginal View of the Bicentenary

Kevin Carmody

I speak to you as one of the indigenous people of this, our vast and sacred ancient land. We in this part of our continent refer to ourselves as Murries.

I have been asked to comment on your Bicentennial. This I will do, though the Truth will no doubt offend you, the European, the ethnic majority.

In 1788, European time, the first small band of European, radical aggressors invaded our lands. They formed a beachhead on the continent's east coast and proceeded from there, by violent and savage means to subjugate the rest of the land, and our people, the Murri inhabitants.

As a Murri person I do not comprehend how you could leave your spiritual and cultural homelands in Europe and intrude here so arrogantly and permanently, without recompense or recognition of our sovereignty.

You are an insensitive and barbaric people.

This undeclared war raged the width and breadth of this continent, and to this day our struggle continues unabated as witnessed by the horrendous statistics of our people's deaths in custody (they are our most recent martyrs for the struggle), look at our infant mortality and health figures, our education and our economic poverty.

We as a nation knew no jails, no private property no standing armies; no leaders; no shackles; no leg irons; no chains; no police, and no whippings of our fellow human beings.

My mother's mother, my great uncles and aunties were forced by you onto reserves, town fringes and missions.

My grandfather, uncles and aunties were delivered up to the hands of these new materialistic, technological savages, whose Creed of Greed blinded them to the basis of their imported Christian theology; i.e. "to love one another, and to do unto others as you would have them do to you".

You have not yet learnt the harmony, balance and gentleness needed to co-exist with the fragile earth as Murries do.

You must display respect and forge a rapport with the Mother earth, as we have done for millennia.

Where is the quality of your existence?

You are a shallow, rootless, hollow people.

Your systems destroy the forests and erode the land to the rivers mouth.

Your actions show your society is savagely barbaric.

You are spiritual paupers.

You must learn to smell the warm honey-scented spring air.

You must learn to experience the beauty and the majesty of the waning autumn moon.

You must learn to imagine a gentle evening's rain upon the desert's flowering red sands.

These things are an intimate part of our Murri Heritage.

Because you are not a Murri you do not understand the essence of the earth. This is your European short-coming. From us you must learn, or your civilisation will destroy this earth.

I as a Murri person find this fate too horrific to contemplate.

You are the ultimate global nomads, whose destructive technological progress and developments, if allowed to proceed

unchecked, will eventually annihilate all humankind.
Is this the legacy to which you wish us, as Murries, to aspire?
You ask us to be thankful and indeed to admire your concept of "progress". This I cannot and will not do, and as my forebears before me resisted this "regression" so too will I.
My culture has given me a pride and a dignity – a sense of awe and humiliation at the majesty and the vastness, the enormity, diversity and sacredness of all Creation.
Please do not delude yourself that I as a Murri am your "Problem" –
You and the Bicentennial are mine.
Thank you.

ABC News Commentary by Kevin Carmody, 26.1.86

Annotations

11-12 **beachhead** strong position on a beach established by an army which has just landed and is preparing to advance and attack – 26 **unabated** as strong as before – 28 **deaths in custody** deaths of prisoners – 34 **shackles** metal rings linked by a chain, used for fastening a prisoner's wrists or ankles together – 34 **leg irons** shackles for a prisoner's legs – 50-51 **to forge a rapport** to establish a relationship – 63 **to wane** (of the moon) to decrease gradually – 68 **heritage** cultural achievements that have been passed on from earlier generations – 79 **to annihilate** to destroy completely – 81-82 **Is this ... aspire?** Do you want us to hope for this? – 89 **awe** feeling of respect combined with fear or wonder – 92 **to delude oneself** *sich täuschen*

Assignments

1. What is the Aboriginal speaker's view of the situation in Australia two years before the Bicentennial? (Inhalt)
2. According to the speaker, what is the fundamental difference between the Aborigines (here: Murries) and the white Australians? (Inhalt)
3. What stylistic and rhetorical devices does the speaker employ to make his speech sound impressive? (Form)
4. Mr Carmody predicts that his "Truth" will offend the white Australians (lines 6-8). Is it an offensive speech? What is your personal reaction to it? (Stellungnahme)
5. Mr Carmody accuses the Whites of destroying this earth with their concept of "progress", which he calls "regression". Do you think he is exaggerating? (Stellungnahme)

Solutions

1. Australia is still occupied by the European invaders, there is still no recompense for the land or recognition of the Aborigines' rightful ownership; the undeclared war continues; statistics show how disadvantaged black Australians are; the white Australians are about to destroy mankind with their concept of progress, etc.
2. The Aborigines
   - are deeply rooted in their religious beliefs
   - have a rich cultural heritage
   - possess the harmony, balance and gentleness needed to co-exist with the fragile earth

– respect the law
– have a deep respect for nature and preserve it
– have great knowledge of the earth and could teach the Whites about it, etc.

The white Australians
– are rootless (left their spiritual and cultural homelands)
– are insensitive, barbaric people
– are materialistically minded; their greed makes them forget their religious principles
– do not respect nature; do not live in harmony with nature
– lack values
– do not understand the essence of the earth, etc.

3. – Sophisticated vocabulary; preference for words of Latin origin (e.g. "to comprehend", "to annihilate", "to proceed", "to aspire", etc.)
– abundant use of adjectives and adverbs (e.g. "radical aggressors", "intrude arrogantly and permanently", etc.)
– complex sentences; predominance of hypotactic sentence structure
– use of adjectives and nouns that are generally not associated with white people (e.g. "insensitive", "barbaric", "rootless", "savages", etc.)
– use of personal pronouns and possessive adjectives to create a distance between the speaker (**I, we**) and his audience (e.g. "**your** Bicentennial", "**you**, the European majority", etc.)
– repetitions (e.g. ll. 32-36: emphatic repetition of "no")
– parallel sentence structure/anaphora (e.g. ll. 60, 62, 64)
– rhetorical questions (e.g. l. 53, ll. 81-82), etc.

By expressing himself in this way, the speaker puts himself on equal terms with the white Australians. He gives the impression of a well-educated, self-confident person who is by no means inferior to white people.

4. Obviously, the speaker wants to provoke his audience. The students might therefore respond on an affective level.

5. The students should discuss the question of whether progress, as understood by white people, necessarily leads to destruction.

Acknowledgements

Vivian Walker: "The Beginning of Life" from *Aboriginal Children's Stories,* brochure

Murray Wilton: "One time we were ..." from *Yuru Ngawarla,* Interview with Murray Wilton by Buck McKenzie and Adele Pring, in: *Australian Short Stories, No. 32,* ed. by Bruce Pascoe, Apollo Bay, Pascoe Publishing Pty Ltd., 1990, p. 69

Buck McKenzie: "When I was little ..." from *Nigger, Nigger*, Interview with Buck McKenzie by Adele Pring, in: *Australian Short Stories, No. 32,* ed. by Bruce Pascoe, Apollo Bay, Pascoe Publishing Pty Ltd., 1990, p. 72

Sally Morgan: "Epilogue" from *Wanamurraganya* by Sally Morgan, South Fremantle, Fremantle Arts Centre Press, 1989, pp. 194-196

Glen Healey Hood: "Racism that stalks WA" from *West Australian*, August 22, 1992, p. 2

Kevin Carmody: "An Aboriginal View of the Bicentenary", ABC News Commentary, 26.1.86, from *ATSIC: Community Aid Abroad Discussion Sheet No 10 – Aborigines and The State*